"Jamie is a genius when it comes to delicious flavor combinations, especially with poke cakes! You are sure to love all of her creative cakes in this cookbook."

—JULIE EVINK, founder of the blog Julie's Eat & Treats

"If you're a fan of poke cake, Jamie has put together an impressive collection of creative variations that are both delicious and fun. Making these recipes is easy...deciding which flavor combo to try first is the real challenge! *The Poke Cake Cookbook* is sure to become your go-to any time you need an effortless dessert for picnics, potlucks or get-togethers."

—SAMANTHA SKAGGS, creator of the blog Five Heart Home
and author of *Real Food Slow Cooker Suppers*

"When I'm looking for delicious food to make, I turn to Jamie. Her recipes are easy, tasty and perfect for all skill levels—recipes that you will want to make again and again!"

—DEB ATTINELLA, founder of the blog Cooking on the Front Burner

"Jamie is always my go-to source for easy dessert recipes. This book is a must-have for your collection!"

—ANDI GLEESON, founder of the blog The Weary Chef

"Jamie has taken a favorite dessert from my childhood and elevated it to an entirely new level! The collection of recipes in *The Poke Cake Cookbook* is innovative, fun and (of course) delicious!"

—MARTHA PESA, founder of the blog A Family Feast

"When it comes to poke cakes, Jamie knows how to do them right! Buy this book and turn your next celebration up a notch!"

—REBECCA HUBBELL, founder of the blog Sugar & Soul

"Jamie definitely knows her poke cakes!"

—MELISSA WILLIAMS, founder of the blog Persnickety Plates

"Jamie is THE master of poke cakes. You will learn so much from the wealth of information in her book. I highly recommend buying it at the first chance you get!"

—NANCY PIRAN, founder of the blog The Bitter Side of Sweet

"If there's one cookbook you need to add to your collection, it is *The Poke Cake Cookbook*. Jamie has made hundreds of recipes and never ceases to wow the crowds!"

—YVONNE FELD, founder of the blog Tried and Tasty

"When it comes to poke cake recipes, Jamie shows us just how creative she can be. This cookbook's inspiring flavors and easy techniques blow the poke cake category wide open!"

—SHERYL BEYER, founder of the blog Lady Behind the Curtain

"Jamie truly knows how to put love into all of her recipes. Buy this book and see the love for yourself!"

—RACHEL FARNSWORTH, cookbook author, blogger at The Stay at Home Chef

"This book is a cake lover's DREAM! It has every flavor you could imagine, and I love the poke cake twist. It's perfect for special occasions or every day, these recipes are sure to become fast favorites. If you love cake, this book is a must-buy!"

—CATHY TROCHELMAN, Lemon Tree Dwelling

the *poke cake* COOKBOOK

75 DELICIOUS CAKE AND FILLING COMBINATIONS

Jamie Sherman

founder of Love Bakes Good Cakes

PAGE STREET
PUBLISHING CO.

PAGE STREET
PUBLISHING CO.

First published in 2017 by

Page Street Publishing Co.

27 Congress Street, Suite 105

Salem, MA 01970

www.pagestreetpublishing.com

Distributed by Macmillan, sales in Canada by The Canadian Manda Group.

21   20   19   18   17   1   2   3   4   5

ISBN-13: 978-1-62414-439-4

ISBN-10: 1-62414-439-X

Library of Congress Control Number: 2017937421

Cover and book design by Page Street Publishing Co.

Photography by Jennifer Blume

Printed and bound in China

FOR THOSE WHO HAVE
ENCOURAGED ME TO DREAM BIG

Contents

EASY AS A-B-C KID-FRIENDLY POKE CAKES 95

IF YOU CAN DREAM IT, YOU CAN ACHIEVE IT 125

INTRODUCTION

On a February afternoon in 2012, I hit the publish button for the very first time and my Love Bakes Good Cakes blog was born. I wasn't really sure what I expected to happen after publishing that first post, but I did know that I had a passion for cooking and baking and the desire to share that passion with anyone and everyone who wanted to read about it.

Gradually, Love Bakes Good Cakes has grown into something bigger than I ever could have imagined. I've had so many amazing opportunities over the past five years—I still sit in awe most days! Not only have I enjoyed creating and sharing recipes, but I cherish the community that goes along with having a food blog. I am humbled that so many people take time out of their day to spend time with me. Whether they're stopping by the blog for a dinner recipe, sharing my posts on Facebook, pinning ideas on Pinterest, sending me an email telling me how much one of my recipes reminds them of their childhood, or just being one of my biggest cheerleaders—I appreciate all of their support. Because of you, I love doing what I do.

Some of the most popular recipes on my blog are the poke cake recipes. I'm not sure if it's the novelty of a "poke cake" or the fact that they are so easy to make and the flavor combinations are almost endless. When presented the opportunity to create a cookbook, I had a few ideas. However, the one that stuck out the most and the one that I knew I wanted to publish was a poke cake cookbook!

I hope through this book you are encouraged to get creative, but more importantly, I hope this cookbook and its recipes help bring friends and families together. For most of us, our fondest memories are of time spent with the ones we love and the good food we share—and what could be sweeter than a poke cake?

Before we get to baking, I invite you to stop by my little part of the Internet where you will find so many more recipes that are family friendly. I've got you covered with healthier meal choices all the way to over-the-top desserts. I would love for you to stop by Love Bakes Good Cakes and say hi. In addition, I hope you enjoy this cookbook; I'm sure you will find a few new family-favorite recipes!

Jamie Sherman

THE CLASSICS YOU KNOW AND LOVE

Kiss boring cakes goodbye!

What would a cake cookbook be without the classics? If you think you love Black Forest Cake (page 13), Pig Pickin' Cake (page 21), Carrot Cake (page 25) or Boston Cream Pie (page 14), wait until you try them all as poke cakes!

black forest poke cake

Put a new twist on the classic Black Forest Cake by turning it into a poke cake! Bursting with chocolate and cherries, this cake is perfect for potlucks or special occasions.

PREP TIME: 10 MINUTES + CHILLING
COOK TIME: 35 MINUTES
YIELD: 18–24 SERVINGS

1 (15.25-oz [432-g]) box dark chocolate cake mix

1 (3.4-oz [96-g]) package chocolate instant pudding mix

2 cups (475 ml) cold milk

1 (10–12-oz [284–340-g]) jar hot chocolate topping

1 (21-oz [595-g]) can cherry pie filling

1 (8-oz [227-g]) tub frozen whipped topping, thawed

Chocolate shavings, for garnish

18–24 maraschino cherries with stems, for garnish

PREPARE and bake the cake according to package directions, using a 13 x 9-inch (33 x 23-cm) cake pan. Let it cool for 15 to 20 minutes. Using the round end of a wooden spoon, poke holes in the cake every ½ inch (1.3 cm) to 1 inch (2.5 cm).

EMPTY the pudding mix into a medium-sized bowl and add the milk. Whisk briskly for 2 minutes or until the pudding is dissolved. Evenly pour over the poked cake, filling the holes as much as possible. Place the covered cake in the refrigerator for 2 to 4 hours or until the pudding is set.

MICROWAVE the hot chocolate topping in a microwave-safe container for 20 to 30 seconds, or until it is easy to pour. Drizzle the topping over the cake. Use the back of a spoon to spread it evenly. Spoon the cherry pie filling evenly over the chocolate layer.

FROST the cake with the whipped topping. Garnish with chocolate shavings and maraschino cherries.

STORE covered in the refrigerator.

boston cream pie poke cake

With just a few common ingredients, you are on your way to a crowd-pleasing dessert. You may never make Boston Cream Pie the regular way ever again!

PREP TIME: 10 MINUTES + CHILLING
COOK TIME: 35 MINUTES
YIELD: 18–24 SERVINGS

1 (15.25-oz [432-g]) box yellow cake mix

2 (3.4-oz [96-g]) packages vanilla instant pudding mix

4 cups (950 ml) cold milk

1 (16-oz [453-g]) can chocolate frosting

PREPARE and bake the cake according to package directions, using a 13 x 9-inch (33 x 23-cm) cake pan. Let it cool for 15 to 20 minutes. Using the round end of a wooden spoon, poke holes in the cake every ½ inch (1.3 cm) to 1 inch (2.5 cm).

EMPTY the pudding mix into a medium-sized bowl and add the milk. Whisk briskly for 2 minutes or until the pudding is dissolved. Evenly pour over the poked cake, filling the holes as much as possible. Place the covered cake in the refrigerator for 2 to 4 hours or until the pudding is set.

MICROWAVE the chocolate frosting in a microwave-safe container for 15 to 20 seconds, or until it is easy to pour. Drizzle the melted frosting over the cake. Use the back of a spoon or an offset spatula to spread it evenly. Refrigerate for at least 2 hours before serving.

STORE covered in the refrigerator.

banana puddin' poke cake

Banana Pudding is a dessert that often shows up at Southern gatherings, and it's absolutely delicious as a poke cake. If you are looking for a dessert that will impress, look no further. This Banana Puddin' Poke Cake always gets rave reviews...be ready to share the recipe!

PREP TIME: 10 MINUTES + CHILLING
COOK TIME: 35 MINUTES
YIELD: 18–24 SERVINGS

1 (15.25-oz [432-g]) box yellow cake mix

2 (3.4-oz [96-g]) packages banana cream instant pudding mix

4 cups (950 ml) cold milk

3–4 medium-sized bananas, peeled and sliced

1 (8-oz [227-g]) tub frozen whipped topping, thawed

24 vanilla wafer cookies, crushed

PREPARE and bake the cake according to package directions, using a 13 x 9-inch (33 x 23-cm) cake pan. Let it cool for 15 to 20 minutes. Using the round end of a wooden spoon, poke holes in the cake every ½ inch (1.3 cm) to 1 inch (2.5 cm).

EMPTY the pudding mix into a medium-sized bowl and add the milk. Whisk briskly for 2 minutes or until the pudding is dissolved. Evenly pour over the poked cake, filling the holes as much as possible. Place the covered cake in the refrigerator for 2 to 4 hours or until the pudding is set.

LAYER the banana slices over the top of the cake. Frost the cake with the whipped topping and garnish with crushed cookies.

STORE covered in the refrigerator.

very vanilla poke cake

You can't go wrong with vanilla! Although this cake is great for any occasion, I love serving it for birthdays and potlucks. This often-underappreciated flavor shows it can easily be the star in this fabulous Very Vanilla Poke Cake.

PREP TIME: 10 MINUTES + CHILLING
COOK TIME: 35 MINUTES
YIELD: 18–24 SERVINGS

1 (15.25-oz [432-g]) box white cake mix

2 (3.4-oz [96-g]) packages vanilla instant pudding mix

4 cups (950 ml) cold milk

1 (16-oz [453-g]) can vanilla frosting

PREPARE and bake the cake according to package directions, using a 13 x 9-inch (33 x 23-cm) cake pan. Let it cool for 15 to 20 minutes. Using the round end of a wooden spoon, poke holes in the cake every ½ inch (1.3 cm) to 1 inch (2.5 cm).

EMPTY the pudding mix into a medium-sized bowl and add the milk. Whisk briskly for 2 minutes or until the pudding is dissolved. Evenly pour over the poked cake, filling the holes as much as possible. Place the covered cake in the refrigerator for 2 to 4 hours or until the pudding is set.

MICROWAVE the vanilla frosting in a microwave-safe container for 15 to 20 seconds, or until it is easy to pour. Drizzle the melted frosting over the cake. Use the back of a spoon or an offset spatula to spread it evenly. Refrigerate for at least 2 hours before serving.

STORE covered in the refrigerator.

pig pickin' poke cake

While this may be a new cake for some people, this classic Southern cake's flavor has nothing to do with pigs or pork! It is often served at pig pickins—or pig pulls or pig roasts—all over the South. Mandarin oranges and pineapple combine in this tasty cake that is a cinch to put together. Great for barbecues and potlucks, this cake is sure to please.

PREP TIME: 10 MINUTES + CHILLING
COOK TIME: 35 MINUTES
YIELD: 18–24 SERVINGS

1 (15.25-oz [432-g]) box golden butter cake mix

¾ cup (180 ml) vegetable oil

4 large eggs

1 (15-oz [425-g]) can Mandarin oranges, undrained

1 (14-oz [397-g]) can sweetened condensed milk

1 (3.4-oz [96-g]) package vanilla instant pudding mix

1 (20-oz [567-g]) can crushed pineapple, undrained

1 (16-oz [453-g]) tub frozen whipped topping, thawed

Additional Mandarin oranges, for garnish

Mint leaves, for garnish

PREHEAT the oven to 350°F (177°C). Spray a 13 x 9-inch (33 x 23-cm) cake pan with cooking spray and set aside.

COMBINE the cake mix, oil and eggs in a large bowl until thoroughly mixed. Add the can of Mandarin oranges (including liquid). Beat until well combined. Pour the batter evenly into the prepared baking pan. Bake for 35 to 40 minutes or until a toothpick inserted near the center of the cake comes out clean. Remove from the oven and let cool for 10 to 15 minutes. With the handle end of a wooden spoon, poke holes all over the cake; make plenty of holes so the filling can soak into the cake.

POUR the sweetened condensed milk over the cake, filling the holes as much as possible.

EMPTY the pudding mix into a medium-sized bowl and add the pineapple with juice. Mix until well combined. Add the whipped topping and mix well. Evenly spread the whipped topping mixture over the poked cake, filling the holes as much as possible. Place the covered cake in the refrigerator for at least 4 hours.

JUST before serving, garnish with extra Mandarin oranges and mint leaves.

STORE covered in the refrigerator.

snowball poke cake

Do you remember those little snack cakes with the chocolate cake, marshmallow frosting and hot pink coconut? They are the inspiration for this Snowball Poke Cake. Relive the good ol' days with this twist on a childhood favorite!

PREP TIME: 10 MINUTES + CHILLING
COOK TIME: 35 MINUTES
YIELD: 18–24 SERVINGS

1 (15.25-oz [432-g]) box chocolate cake mix

2 (3.4-oz [96-g]) packages chocolate instant pudding mix

4 cups (950 ml) cold milk

2 (7-oz [198-g] each) jars marshmallow creme

1½ cups (128 g) sweetened coconut flakes

Pink food coloring

PREPARE and bake the cake according to package directions, using a 13 x 9-inch (33 x 23-cm) cake pan. Let it cool for 15 to 20 minutes. Using the round end of a wooden spoon, poke holes in the cake every ½ inch (1.3 cm) to 1 inch (2.5 cm).

EMPTY the pudding mix into a medium-sized bowl and add the milk. Whisk briskly for 2 minutes or until the pudding is dissolved. Evenly pour over the poked cake, filling the holes as much as possible. Place the covered cake in the refrigerator for 2 to 4 hours or until the pudding is set.

PLACE dollops of the marshmallow creme over the cake. Use the back of a spoon or an offset spatula to spread it evenly in a large ziptop bag. Put the coconut and a few drops of pink food coloring. Seal the bag and shake until the coconut is uniformly colored. Evenly spread the coconut over the cake. Refrigerate for at least 2 hours before serving.

STORE covered in the refrigerator.

carrot cake poke cake

Just like the classic cake, this poke cake version starts with a boxed carrot cake mix and is topped off with a luscious cream cheese topping. As an added bonus, you'll find this cake poked with a creamy caramel sauce. If you're looking for a great springtime or Easter dessert, give this Carrot Cake Poke Cake a try. It's a fun twist on the classic cake.

PREP TIME: 10 MINUTES + CHILLING
COOK TIME: 35 MINUTES
YIELD: 18-24 SERVINGS

1 (15.25–21.41-oz [432–607-g]) box carrot cake mix

1 (14-oz [397-g]) can sweetened condensed milk

1 cup (250 ml) caramel topping

1 (8-oz [227-g]) package cream cheese, softened

1 (16-oz [453-g]) tub frozen whipped topping, thawed

½ cup (62 g) powdered sugar

½ tsp vanilla extract

Additional caramel topping, for garnish

½ cup (78 g) toffee bits, for garnish

PREPARE and bake the cake according to package directions, using a 13 x 9-inch (33 x 23-cm) cake pan. Let it cool for 15 to 20 minutes. Using the round end of a wooden spoon, poke holes in the cake every ½ inch (1.3 cm) to 1 inch (2.5 cm).

COMBINE the sweetened condensed milk and caramel topping in a medium bowl. Pour the caramel mixture over the top of the cake, filling the holes as much as possible. Let the cake cool completely.

BEAT the cream cheese, whipped topping, powdered sugar and vanilla extract in a large bowl until well combined. Spread the cream cheese mixture over the cake. Drizzle the additional caramel topping over the cream cheese mixture. Sprinkle the toffee bits on top. Refrigerate for at least 2 hours before serving.

STORE covered in the refrigerator.

snickerdoodle poke cake

Snickerdoodle...isn't that such a fun thing to say? With Snickerdoodles being one of my favorite cookies, I wanted to make a Snickerdoodle version of the poke cake. If you're a fan of vanilla and cinnamon, then this cake is for you!

PREP TIME: 10 MINUTES + CHILLING
COOK TIME: 35 MINUTES
YIELD: 18-24 SERVINGS

1 (15.25-oz [432-g]) box white cake mix

1 cup (240 ml) milk

½ cup (1 stick [113 g]) butter, melted and cooled

3 large eggs

3 tsp (15 ml) vanilla extract, divided

2 tsp (5 g) ground cinnamon, divided

1 (3.4-oz [96-g]) package vanilla instant pudding mix

2 cups (475 ml) cold milk

½ cup (1 stick [113 g]) butter, softened

3-4 cups (390-520 g) powdered sugar

¼ cup (60 ml) heavy cream, half & half or milk

PREHEAT the oven to 350°F (177°C). Spray a 13 x 9-inch (33 x 23-cm) cake pan with cooking spray and set aside.

COMBINE the cake mix, milk, melted butter, eggs, 2 teaspoons (10 ml) vanilla extract and 1 teaspoon ground cinnamon in a large bowl until thoroughly mixed. Pour the batter evenly into the prepared baking pan. Bake for 30 to 35 minutes or until a toothpick inserted near the center of the cake comes out clean. Remove from the oven and let cool 10 to 15 minutes. With the handle end of a wooden spoon, poke holes all over the cake; make plenty of holes so the filling can soak into the cake.

EMPTY the pudding mix into a medium-sized bowl and add the milk. Whisk briskly for 2 minutes or until the pudding is dissolved. Evenly pour over the poked cake, filling the holes as much as possible. Place covered cake in the refrigerator for 2 to 4 hours or until the pudding is set.

BEAT the softened butter, powdered sugar, heavy cream, 1 teaspoon vanilla extract and remaining 1 teaspoon cinnamon in a large bowl until the frosting is light and fluffy. Spread the frosting over the cake. Refrigerate for at least 4 hours before serving.

STORE covered in the refrigerator.

red velvet poke cake

This **Red Velvet Poke Cake** is an easy addition to your holiday table. It's great for Valentine's Day, 4th of July, Labor Day, Christmas—or any day you are craving a luscious treat. Switch out the sprinkles to match the holiday.

PREP TIME: 10 MINUTES + CHILLING
COOK TIME: 35 MINUTES
YIELD: 18–24 SERVINGS

1 (18.25-oz [517-g]) box red velvet cake mix

1 (3.4–3.56-oz [96–101-g]) package white chocolate instant pudding mix

2 cups (475 ml) milk

4 oz (113 g) cream cheese, softened

1 (8-oz [227-g]) tub frozen whipped topping, thawed

¼ cup (31 g) powdered sugar

¼ tsp vanilla extract

Seasonal sprinkles or nonpareils (optional)

PREPARE and bake the cake according to package directions, using a 13 x 9-inch (33 x 23-cm) cake pan. Let it cool for 15 to 20 minutes. Using the round end of a wooden spoon, poke holes in the cake every ½ inch (1.3 cm) to 1 inch (2.5 cm).

EMPTY the pudding mix into a medium-sized bowl and add the milk. Whisk briskly for 2 minutes or until the pudding is dissolved. Evenly pour over the poked cake, filling the holes as much as possible. Place the covered cake in the refrigerator for 2 to 4 hours or until the pudding is set.

MIX the cream cheese, whipped topping, powdered sugar and vanilla in a large bowl until well combined and the mixture is light and fluffy. Spread over the cake. Refrigerate for at least 4 hours before serving.

TOP the cake with the sprinkles or nonpareils just before serving.

STORE covered in the refrigerator.

s'mores poke cake

Skip the bonfire with this S'mores Poke Cake! Here, boxed chocolate cake mix is topped with marshmallow, graham crackers and even more chocolate.

PREP TIME: 10 MINUTES + CHILLING
COOK TIME: 35 MINUTES
YIELD: 18–24 SERVINGS

1 (15.25-oz [432-g]) box chocolate cake mix

1 (14-oz [397-g]) can sweetened condensed milk

1¼ cups (380 g) hot fudge topping, divided

1 (7-oz [198-g]) jar marshmallow creme

5–6 graham crackers, coarsely chopped

1 cup (57 g) mini marshmallows

½ cup (84 g) mini chocolate chips

PREPARE and bake the cake according to package directions, using a 13 x 9-inch (33 x 23-cm) cake pan. Let it cool for 15 to 20 minutes. Using the round end of a wooden spoon, poke holes in the cake every ½ inch (1.3 cm) to 1 inch (2.5 cm).

POUR the sweetened condensed milk over the cake, filling the holes as much as possible. Microwave 1 cup (304 g) hot fudge sauce in a microwave-safe container in 15-second intervals until it is pourable. Drizzle the hot fudge sauce over the cake, filling the holes as much as possible.

HEAT the marshmallow creme in a microwave-safe container for 15 seconds to soften it. Spread the marshmallow creme over the cake.

TOP with graham crackers, mini marshmallows and mini chocolate chips. Refrigerate for at least 4 hours before serving. Drizzle with an additional ¼ cup (76 g) hot fudge topping just before serving.

STORE covered in the refrigerator.

NOTE: If you like toasty marshmallows, you can use a kitchen torch to lightly toast your marshmallows. Use caution when using a kitchen torch.

reese's poke cake

Chocolate and peanut butter are made for each other—and this Reese's Poke Cake just solidifies that fact. A chocolate cake mix is poked with a creamy peanut butter pudding mix. It includes a layer of chocolate and whipped topping before being topped with plenty of peanut butter cups.

PREP TIME: 10 MINUTES + CHILLING
COOK TIME: 35 MINUTES
YIELD: 18–24 SERVINGS

1 (15.25-oz [432-g]) box chocolate cake mix

1 (3.4-oz [96-g]) package vanilla instant pudding mix

2 cups (475 ml) cold milk

1½ cups (270 g) creamy peanut butter, divided

1 (16-oz [453-g]) can chocolate frosting

1 (8-oz [227-g]) tub frozen whipped topping, thawed

25 Reese's peanut butter cup miniatures, unwrapped and roughly chopped

PREPARE and bake the cake according to package directions, using a 13 x 9-inch (33 x 23-cm) cake pan. Let the cake cool for 15 to 20 minutes. Using the round end of a wooden spoon, poke holes in the cake every ½ inch (1.3 cm) to 1 inch (2.5 cm).

EMPTY the pudding mix into a medium-sized bowl and add the milk. Whisk briskly for 2 minutes or until the pudding is dissolved. Add ½ cup (90 g) of peanut butter and whisk until well combined. Evenly pour the pudding mixture over the cake, filling the holes as much as possible.

MICROWAVE the chocolate frosting in a microwave-safe container for 15 to 20 seconds, or until it is easy to pour. Drizzle the melted frosting over the cake. Use the back of a spoon or an offset spatula to spread it evenly. Let the cake cool completely.

WHISK together the remaining 1 cup (180 g) peanut butter and whipped topping in a large bowl. Spread over the cake. Top with peanut butter cups. Refrigerate for at least 4 hours before serving.

STORE covered in the refrigerator.

hummingbird poke cake

Impress your friends with this updated Southern classic! This banana-pineapple spice cake is poked with banana pudding and topped with a dreamy cream cheese spread, then sprinkled with nuts.

PREP TIME: 10 MINUTES + CHILLING
COOK TIME: 35 MINUTES
YIELD: 18-24 SERVINGS

1 (15.25-oz [432-g]) box yellow cake mix

1 cup (230 g) mashed ripe bananas

1 (8-oz [227-g]) can crushed pineapple, undrained

¼ cup (60 ml) vegetable oil

¼ cup (60 ml) water

1 tsp ground cinnamon

3 large eggs

1 (3.4-oz [96-g]) package banana cream instant pudding mix

2 cups (475 ml) cold milk

½ cup (1 stick [113 g]) butter, softened

8 oz (227 g) cream cheese, softened

1 tsp vanilla extract

4 cups (520 g) powdered sugar

½ cup (55 g) chopped pecans

PREHEAT the oven to 350°F (177°C). Spray a 13 x 9-inch (33 x 23-cm) cake pan with cooking spray and set aside.

MIX the cake mix, bananas, pineapple, oil, water, cinnamon and eggs in a large bowl until well combined. Pour the batter evenly into the prepared baking pan. Bake for 27 to 32 minutes or until a toothpick inserted near the center of the cake comes out clean. Remove from the oven, let cool for 10 to 15 minutes. With the handle end of a wooden spoon, poke holes all over the cake; make plenty of holes so the pudding can soak into the cake.

EMPTY the pudding mix into a medium-sized bowl and add the milk. Whisk briskly for 2 minutes or until the pudding is dissolved. Evenly pour over the poked cake, filling the holes as much as possible. Place the covered cake in the refrigerator for 2 to 4 hours or until the pudding is set.

COMBINE the butter, cream cheese, vanilla extract and powdered sugar in a large bowl with an electric mixer until light and fluffy. Spread the cream cheese mixture over the top of the cake. Garnish with pecans. Refrigerate for 4 hours before serving.

STORE covered in the refrigerator.

new york cheesecake poke cake

If you thought New York Cheesecake was decadent, wait until you try this poke cake version. A white cake mix poked with a rich and creamy no-bake cheesecake filling, topped off with cherries. Grab a fork!

PREP TIME: 10 MINUTES + CHILLING
COOK TIME: 35 MINUTES
YIELD: 18–24 SERVINGS

1 (15.25-oz [432-g]) box white cake mix

2 (8-oz [240-g]) packages cream cheese, softened

⅔ cup (132 g) granulated sugar

1 (16-oz [453-g]) tub frozen whipped topping, thawed

1–2 (21-oz [595-g]) cans cherry pie filling

PREPARE and bake the cake according to package directions, using a 13 x 9-inch (33 x 23-cm) cake pan. Let the cake cool for 15 to 20 minutes. Using the round end of a wooden spoon, poke holes in the cake every ½ inch (1.3 cm) to 1 inch (2.5 cm).

PLACE the cream cheese and sugar in a large bowl and beat with an electric mixer until smooth. Fold in the whipped topping. Evenly pour over the poked cake, filling the holes as much as possible. Spread the cherry pie filling over the frosting. Refrigerate for at least 4 hours before serving.

STORE covered in the refrigerator.

mississippi mud poke cake

This Southern classic sheet cake gets an update. Chocolate cake is poked with marshmallow creme, chocolate icing and plenty of toasted pecans.

PREP TIME: 10 MINUTES + CHILLING
COOK TIME: 35 MINUTES
YIELD: 18–24 SERVINGS

1 (15.25-oz [432-g]) box chocolate cake mix

1 (14-oz [397-g]) can sweetened condensed milk

2 (7-oz [198-g]) containers marshmallow creme

½ cup (1 stick [113 g]) butter

¼ cup (28 g) unsweetened cocoa powder

⅓ cup (80 ml) milk

4 cups (520 g) powdered sugar

1 cup (110 g) toasted pecans

PREPARE and bake the cake according to package directions, using a 13 x 9-inch (33 x 23-cm) cake pan. Let the cake cool for 15 to 20 minutes. Using the round end of a wooden spoon, poke holes in the cake every ½ inch (1.3 cm) to 1 inch (2.5 cm).

BEAT the sweetened condensed milk and marshmallow creme in a large bowl until well combined. Evenly pour over the poked cake, filling the holes as much as possible.

HEAT the butter in a medium saucepan over low heat until melted. Whisk in the cocoa powder and milk. Stirring constantly, bring the mixture just to a boil; immediately remove from the heat and whisk in the powdered sugar until thickened and smooth. Pour the icing over the top of the marshmallow layer and carefully spread the icing to the edges of the pan using the back of a spoon or an offset spatula. Sprinkle pecans evenly over the top. Allow the cake to cool completely before serving.

STORE covered in the refrigerator.

EASY CHOCOLATE POKE CAKES TO DIE FOR

Calling all chocolate fans: This is the chapter for you!

When I sat down to think about what kinds of recipes I wanted to include in this cookbook, I quickly realized that not only did I need a chocolate chapter, I could have easily written a poke cake book with only chocolate recipes! Because they all feature chocolate, this chapter shares some of my very favorite poke cake recipes. In this section, you'll find everything from over-the-top chocolate in my Death by Chocolate Poke Cake (page 41), to just a taste of chocolate in my Love Potion #9 Poke Cake (page 63)...with varying levels of chocolate heaven in between.

death by chocolate poke cake

What's a person to do when they want chocolate? Go all out, of course! I seriously don't think I could have stuffed much more chocolate into this cake without needing some sort of resuscitation! And we're not talking about any kind of chocolate here folks...when you have a serious chocolate deprivation, only the dark stuff will do.

PREP TIME: 10 MINUTES + CHILLING
COOK TIME: 35 MINUTES
YIELD: 18–24 SERVINGS

1 (15.25-oz [432-g]) box dark chocolate cake mix

2 boxes (3.56 oz [101-g]) instant Hershey's Special Dark Chocolate Pudding mix, divided

4 cups (950 ml) milk, divided

1 (12.8-oz [363-g]) jar dark chocolate topping

1 (8-oz [227-g]) tub frozen whipped topping, thawed

1 (6.8 oz [190-g]) dark chocolate candy bar, chopped

PREPARE and bake the cake according to package directions, using a 13 x 9-inch (33 x 23-cm) cake pan. Let the cake cool for 15 to 20 minutes. Using the round end of a wooden spoon, poke holes in the cake every ½ inch (1.3 cm) to 1 inch (2.5 cm).

EMPTY one package of pudding mix into a medium-sized bowl and add 2 cups (475 ml) of milk. Whisk briskly for 2 minutes or until the pudding is dissolved. Evenly pour over the poked cake, filling the holes as much as possible. Microwave the chocolate topping, with the lid off, for about 45 seconds or until it pours easily. Pour the chocolate topping evenly over the cake. Place the covered cake in the refrigerator for 2 to 4 hours or until the pudding is set.

COMBINE the second package of pudding mix with the remaining milk in a medium bowl. Carefully fold in the whipped topping. Spread the mixture evenly over the top of the cake. Sprinkle the chopped candy bar over the top. Refrigerate for at least 4 hours before serving.

STORE covered in the refrigerator.

NOTE: I recommend using Hershey's for the chocolate products used in this recipe, in particular for the pudding mix, but if you cannot find it, you may substitute any instant chocolate pudding in its place.

turtle poke cake

Devil's food cake with plenty of caramel, pecans—and yes, more chocolate. The flavors in this recipe perfectly complement each other for a dessert that will have friends and family raving!

PREP TIME: 10 MINUTES + CHILLING
COOK TIME: 35 MINUTES
YIELD: 18-24 SERVINGS

1 (15.25-oz [432-g]) box chocolate cake mix

1 (14-oz [397-g]) can sweetened condensed milk

1 (14-oz [397-g]) jar caramel topping

1 (16-oz [453-g]) can chocolate frosting

1 cup (110 g) chopped pecans

½ cup (84 g) mini chocolate chips

Additional caramel sauce, for drizzling

PREPARE and bake the cake according to package directions, using a 13 x 9-inch (33 x 23-cm) cake pan. Let the cake cool for 15 to 20 minutes. Using the round end of a wooden spoon, poke holes in the cake every ½ inch (1.3 cm) to 1 inch (2.5 cm).

COMBINE the sweetened condensed milk and caramel topping in a medium bowl. Whisk briskly for 1 minute or until the mixture is well combined. Evenly pour over the poked cake, filling the holes as much as possible. Place the cake in the refrigerator for about 1 hour.

REMOVE the cake from the refrigerator. Spread the chocolate frosting over the cake. Use the back of a spoon or an offset spatula to spread it evenly. Sprinkle the chopped pecans and mini chocolate chips over the frosting. Drizzle with additional caramel sauce. Refrigerate for at least 2 hours before serving.

STORE covered in the refrigerator.

german chocolate poke cake

How do you take a classic cake and make it better? By making it into a poke cake! This chocolate cake is poked with chocolate pudding and topped off with a coconut-pecan frosting. You may never want to eat German chocolate cake any other way!

PREP TIME: 10 MINUTES + CHILLING
COOK TIME: 35 MINUTES
YIELD: 18–24 SERVINGS

1 (15.25-oz [432-g]) box German chocolate cake mix

1 (3.4-oz [96-g]) package chocolate instant pudding mix

2 cups (475 ml) cold milk

1 (16-oz [453-g]) can coconut-pecan frosting

PREPARE and bake the cake according to package directions, using a 13 x 9-inch (33 x 23-cm) cake pan. Let the cake cool for 15 to 20 minutes. Using the round end of a wooden spoon, poke holes in the cake every ½ inch (1.3 cm) to 1 inch (2.5 cm).

EMPTY the pudding mix into a medium-sized bowl and add the milk. Whisk briskly for 2 minutes or until the pudding is dissolved. Evenly pour over the poked cake, filling the holes as much as possible. Place the covered cake in the refrigerator for 2 to 4 hours or until the pudding is set.

SPREAD the coconut-pecan frosting over the cake. Use the back of a spoon or an offset spatula to spread it evenly. Refrigerate for at least 2 hours before serving.

STORE covered in the refrigerator.

better than sex poke cake

What's in a name? This cake is said to elicit the same feelings of arousal and satisfaction as having sex. You may know it by other popular names like Better than Anything Cake or Better than Robert Redford Cake. Let's just call it good!

PREP TIME: 10 MINUTES + CHILLING
COOK TIME: 35 MINUTES
YIELD: 18–24 SERVINGS

1 (15.25-oz [432-g]) box devil's food cake mix

1 (14-oz [397-g]) can sweetened condensed milk

1 (14-oz [397-g]) jar caramel topping

1 (8-oz [227-g]) tub frozen whipped topping, thawed

3 (1.4-oz [40-g]) bars chocolate-covered toffee, chopped

PREPARE and bake the cake according to package directions, using a 13 x 9-inch (33 x 23-cm) cake pan. Let the cake cool for 15 to 20 minutes. Using the round end of a wooden spoon, poke holes in the cake every ½ inch (1.3 cm) to 1 inch (2.5 cm).

PLACE the sweetened condensed milk and caramel topping in a large bowl. Whisk briskly for 1 minute or until thoroughly combined. Evenly pour the mixture over the poked cake, filling the holes as much as possible.

SPREAD the whipped topping evenly over the cake. Sprinkle with chopped chocolate-covered toffee bars. Refrigerate for at least 2 hours before serving.

STORE covered in the refrigerator.

chocolate-covered strawberry poke cake

Strawberries and chocolate were made for each other! This makes a great Valentine's Day cake.

PREP TIME: 10 MINUTES + CHILLING
COOK TIME: 35 MINUTES
YIELD: 18-24 SERVINGS

1 (15.25-oz [432-g]) box chocolate cake mix

1 (3.4-oz [96-g]) package chocolate instant pudding mix

2 cups (475 ml) cold milk

1 (21-oz [595-g]) can strawberry pie filling

1 (16-oz [453-g]) can chocolate frosting

Fresh strawberries, for garnish

Chocolate curls, for garnish

PREPARE and bake the cake according to package directions, using a 13 x 9-inch (33 x 23-cm) cake pan. Let the cake cool for 15 to 20 minutes. Using the round end of a wooden spoon, poke holes in the cake every ½ inch (1.3 cm) to 1 inch (2.5 cm).

EMPTY the pudding mix into a medium-sized bowl and add the milk. Whisk briskly for 2 minutes or until the pudding is dissolved. Evenly pour over the poked cake, filling the holes as much as possible. Evenly spread the strawberry pie filling over the cake. Place covered cake in the refrigerator for 2 to 4 hours or until the pudding is set.

MICROWAVE the chocolate frosting in a microwave-safe container for 15 to 20 seconds, or until it is easy to pour. Drizzle the melted frosting over the cake. Use the back of a spoon or an offset spatula to spread it evenly. Refrigerate for at least 2 hours before serving. Garnish with fresh strawberries and chocolate curls.

STORE covered in the refrigerator.

chocolate razmatazz poke cake

This decadent cake combines chocolate and raspberry flavors in a poke cake that just begs to be shared!

PREP TIME: 10 MINUTES + CHILLING
COOK TIME: 35 MINUTES
YIELD: 18–24 SERVINGS

1 (15.25-oz [432-g]) box chocolate cake mix

1 (3-oz [85-g]) package raspberry gelatin mix

2 cups (475 ml) hot water

1 (21-oz [595-g]) can raspberry pie filling

1 (16-oz [453-g]) can chocolate frosting

Fresh raspberries, for garnish

Fresh mint leaves, for garnish

PREPARE and bake the cake according to package directions, using a 13 x 9-inch (33 x 23-cm) cake pan. Let the cake cool for 15 to 20 minutes. Using the round end of a wooden spoon, poke holes in the cake every ½ inch (1.3 cm) to 1 inch (2.5 cm).

EMPTY the gelatin into a medium-sized bowl and add the water. Whisk briskly for 2 minutes or until the gelatin is dissolved. Evenly pour over the poked cake, filling the holes as much as possible. Spread the pie filling evenly over the cake. Place the covered cake in the refrigerator for 2 to 4 hours or until the gelatin is set.

MICROWAVE the chocolate frosting in a microwave-safe container for 15 to 20 seconds, or until it is easy to pour. Drizzle the melted frosting over the top of the cake. Use the back of a spoon or an offset spatula to spread it evenly. Refrigerate for at least 2 hours before serving. Garnish the cake with fresh raspberries and mint leaves.

STORE covered in the refrigerator.

See photo on page 38.

samoa poke cake

You don't have to wait for those cookie boxes to show up at your door to make this Samoa Poke Cake! Get all of the flavors you love in this recipe spin. A butter cake is poked with sweet, creamy caramel sauce and topped with chocolate, coconut and a drizzle of extra caramel.

PREP TIME: 10 MINUTES + CHILLING
COOK TIME: 35 MINUTES
YIELD: 18–24 SERVINGS

1 (15.25-oz [432-g]) box butter cake mix

1 (10–14-oz [284–397-g]) jar caramel sauce, divided

1 (14-oz [397-g]) can sweetened condensed milk

1 (16-oz [453-g]) can chocolate frosting

1 cup (85 g) toasted coconut

PREPARE and bake the cake according to package directions, using a 13 x 9-inch (33 x 23-cm) cake pan. Let the cake cool for 15 to 20 minutes. Using the round end of a wooden spoon, poke holes in the cake every ½ inch (1.3 cm) to 1 inch (2.5 cm).

SET aside ¼ cup (82 g) of caramel sauce. Place the remaining caramel sauce in a large bowl with the sweetened condensed milk. Mix well. Evenly pour the caramel mixture over the poked cake, filling the holes as much as possible. Place the covered cake in the refrigerator for 2 to 4 hours.

MICROWAVE the chocolate frosting in a microwave-safe container for 15 to 20 seconds, or until it is easy to pour. Drizzle the melted frosting over the top of the cake. Use the back of a spoon or an offset spatula to spread it evenly. Evenly sprinkle with toasted coconut. Drizzle with the reserved caramel sauce. Refrigerate for at least 2 hours before serving.

STORE covered in the refrigerator.

white chocolate raspberry poke cake

White chocolate and raspberry make a great pair. A white cake is poked with white chocolate pudding and topped with a raspberry filling and whipped topping. White chocolate curls, fresh raspberries and mint leaves garnish this spectacular cake. It is perfect for a ladies' luncheon, a baby shower or birthdays.

PREP TIME: 10 MINUTES + CHILLING
COOK TIME: 35 MINUTES
YIELD: 18–24 SERVINGS

---

1 (15.25-oz [432-g]) box white cake mix

1 (3.4-oz [96-g]) package white chocolate instant pudding mix

2 cups (475 ml) cold milk

1 (21-oz [595-g]) can raspberry pie filling

1 (8-oz [227-g]) tub frozen whipped topping, thawed

White chocolate curls, for garnish

Fresh raspberries, for garnish

Fresh mint leaves, for garnish

PREPARE and bake the cake according to package directions, using a 13 x 9-inch (33 x 23-cm) cake pan. Let the cake cool for 15 to 20 minutes. Using the round end of a wooden spoon, poke holes in the cake every ½ inch (1.3 cm) to 1 inch (2.5 cm).

EMPTY the pudding mix into a medium-sized bowl and add the milk. Whisk briskly for 2 minutes or until the pudding is dissolved. Evenly pour over the poked cake, filling the holes as much as possible. Evenly spread the pie filling over the top. Spread the whipped topping over the pie filling. Place the covered cake in the refrigerator for 2 to 4 hours or until the pudding is set.

JUST before serving, garnish with chocolate curls, fresh raspberries and mint leaves.

STORE covered in the refrigerator.

chocolate mint poke cake

One of life's greatest combos—chocolate and mint. In this recipe, a chocolate cake is poked with chocolate pudding and topped off with hot fudge sauce, a minty whipped topping and mint candies.

PREP TIME: 10 MINUTES + CHILLING
COOK TIME: 35 MINUTES
YIELD: 18–24 SERVINGS

1 (15.25-oz [432-g]) box chocolate cake mix

1 (3.4-oz [96-g]) package chocolate instant pudding mix

2 cups (475 ml) cold milk

1 (12-oz [340-g]) jar hot fudge topping

1 (8-oz [227-g]) tub frozen whipped topping, thawed

¼ tsp peppermint extract

Green food coloring (optional)

12 Andes mints, chopped

Additional hot fudge sauce, for drizzling

PREPARE and bake the cake according to package directions, using a 13 x 9-inch (33 x 23-cm) cake pan. Let the cake cool for 15 to 20 minutes. Using the round end of a wooden spoon, poke holes in the cake every ½ inch (1.3 cm) to 1 inch (2.5 cm).

EMPTY the pudding mix into a medium-sized bowl and add the milk. Whisk briskly for 2 minutes or until the pudding is dissolved. Evenly pour over the poked cake, filling the holes as much as possible. Microwave the hot fudge topping, with the lid off, for about 45 seconds or until it pours easily. Pour the hot fudge topping evenly over the top of the cake. Let the cake cool completely.

MIX the whipped topping, peppermint extract and green food coloring (if desired) in a large bowl just until combined. Spread the mixture over the cake. Top with chopped Andes mints and a drizzle of hot fudge sauce. Refrigerate for at least 2 hours before serving.

STORE covered in the refrigerator.

mexican chocolate poke cake

It's easy to doctor up a chocolate cake mix to make this Mexican Chocolate Poke Cake. Adding cinnamon to the cake batter, and poking it with chocolate pudding, creates an awesome base for the decadent dulce de leche and cream cheese mixture that tops the cake.

PREP TIME: 10 MINUTES + CHILLING
COOK TIME: 35 MINUTES
YIELD: 18-24 SERVINGS

1 (15.25-oz [432-g]) box chocolate cake mix

1½ (4 g) tsp ground cinnamon, divided

1 (3.4-oz [96-g]) package chocolate instant pudding mix

2 cups (475 ml) cold milk

1 (13.4-oz [380-g]) can dulce de leche

1 (8-oz [227-g]) package cream cheese

½ cup (125 ml) heavy whipping cream

Chocolate curls, for garnish

PREPARE and bake the cake according to package directions, adding 1 teaspoon of ground cinnamon to the batter and using a 13 x 9-inch (33 x 23-cm) cake pan. Let the cake cool for 15 to 20 minutes. Using the round end of a wooden spoon, poke holes in the cake every ½ inch (1.3 cm) to 1 inch (2.5 cm).

EMPTY the pudding mix into a medium-sized bowl and add the milk along with the remaining ½ teaspoon ground cinnamon. Whisk briskly for 2 minutes or until the pudding is dissolved. Evenly pour over the poked cake, filling the holes as much as possible. Place the covered cake in the refrigerator for 2 to 4 hours or until the pudding is set.

BEAT the dulce de leche and cream cheese on high speed with an electric mixer in a large bowl until well blended and smooth. Scrape down the sides of the bowl. Beat in the whipping cream until stiff peaks form. Spread the frosting over the cake. Just before serving, garnish with chocolate curls.

STORE covered in the refrigerator.

chunky monkey poke cake

Bananas, chocolate and walnuts are what this cake is all about!

PREP TIME: 10 MINUTES + CHILLING
COOK TIME: 37–43 MINUTES
YIELD: 18–24 SERVINGS

1 (15.25-oz [432-g]) box yellow cake mix

2 very ripe bananas, mashed

1 cup (180 g) chocolate chips

1 (3.4-oz [96-g]) package banana cream instant pudding mix

2 cups (475 ml) cold milk

1 (16-oz [453-g]) can chocolate frosting

¾ cup (83 g) chopped walnuts

PREHEAT the oven to 350°F (177°C). Spray a 13 x 9-inch (33 x 23-cm) cake pan with cooking spray and set aside.

PREPARE the cake according to package directions, adding the bananas and chocolate chips. Beat until well combined. Pour batter evenly into the prepared baking pan. Bake for 37 to 43 minutes or until a toothpick inserted near the center of the cake comes out clean. Remove from the oven and let cool, 10 to 15 minutes. With the handle end of a wooden spoon, poke holes all over the cake; make plenty of holes so the filling can soak into the cake.

EMPTY the pudding mix into a medium-sized bowl and add the milk. Whisk briskly for 2 minutes or until the pudding is dissolved. Evenly pour over the poked cake, filling the holes as much as possible. Place the covered cake in the refrigerator for 2 to 4 hours or until the pudding is set.

MICROWAVE the chocolate frosting in a microwave-safe container for 15 to 20 seconds, or until it is easy to pour. Drizzle the melted frosting over the cake. Use the back of a spoon or an offset spatula to spread it evenly. Sprinkle with walnuts. Refrigerate for at least 4 hours before serving.

STORE covered in the refrigerator.

peppermint mocha poke cake

In this holiday favorite, coffee amplifies the chocolate cake to the next level, while the peppermint pudding brings a refreshing and cool element. Kick it up with a layer of hot fudge before topping it with a thick mousse-like chocolate topping and peppermint candies.

PREP TIME: 10 MINUTES + CHILLING
COOK TIME: 35 MINUTES
YIELD: 18-24 SERVINGS

1 (15.25-oz [432-g]) box chocolate cake mix

Strong brewed coffee (enough to substitute for amount of water listed in cake mix directions)

1 (3.4-oz [96-g]) package vanilla instant pudding mix

1 tsp peppermint extract

3 cups (700 ml) cold milk, divided

1 (11-oz [312-g]) jar hot fudge topping

1 (3.4-oz [96-g]) package chocolate instant pudding mix

1 (8-oz [227-g]) tub frozen whipped topping, thawed

½ cup (68 g) peppermint candies, crushed

Soft peppermint candies, unwrapped

PREPARE and bake the cake according to package directions, substituting coffee for the water and using a 13 x 9-inch (33 x 23-cm) cake pan. Let the cake cool for 15 to 20 minutes. Using the round end of a wooden spoon, poke holes in the cake every ½ inch (1.3 cm) to 1 inch (2.5 cm).

EMPTY the vanilla pudding mix into a medium-sized bowl and add 2 cups (475 ml) of milk. Add 1 teaspoon of peppermint extract. Whisk briskly for 2 minutes or until the pudding is dissolved. Evenly pour over the poked cake, filling the holes as much as possible. Place the covered cake in the refrigerator for 2 to 4 hours or until the pudding is set.

MICROWAVE the hot fudge topping, with the lid off, for about 45 seconds or until it pours easily. Pour the topping evenly over the cake. Refrigerate for at least 2 hours before serving.

EMPTY the chocolate pudding package into a medium-sized bowl and add the remaining 1 cup (240 ml) of milk. Whisk briskly for 2 minutes or until the pudding is dissolved. Fold in the whipped topping and crushed peppermint candies until well combined. Evenly spread the whipped topping mixture over the cake. Refrigerate for at least 4 hours before serving. Just before serving, garnish with soft peppermint candies.

STORE covered in the refrigerator.

NOTE: If you have trouble finding soft peppermint candies for the topping, try searching for Bob's Sweet Stripes Soft Peppermint Balls.

love potion #9 poke cake

A luscious and decadent poke cake perfect for the one you love! In this poke cake, amp up a white cake mix with raspberry gelatin, hot chocolate topping, whipped topping and plenty of fresh raspberries and chocolate shavings.

PREP TIME: 10 MINUTES + CHILLING
COOK TIME: 35 MINUTES
YIELD: 18–24 SERVINGS

1 (15.25-oz [432-g]) box white cake mix

1 (3-oz [85-g]) package raspberry gelatin mix

1 cup (240 ml) boiling water

½ cup (120 ml) cold water

1 (10–12-oz [284–340-g]) jar hot chocolate topping

1 (8-oz [227-g]) tub frozen whipped topping, thawed

1 pint (473 g) fresh raspberries

Chocolate shavings

PREPARE and bake the cake according to package directions, using a 13 x 9-inch (33 x 23-cm) cake pan. Let the cake cool for 15 to 20 minutes. Using a meat fork or wooden skewer, poke holes in the cake every ½ inch (1.3 cm) to 1 inch (2.5 cm).

EMPTY the gelatin into a medium-sized bowl and add the boiling water. Stir briskly for 2 minutes or until the gelatin is dissolved. Mix in the cold water. Evenly pour the gelatin over the poked cake. Place the covered cake in the refrigerator for 2 to 4 hours or until the gelatin is set.

MICROWAVE the hot chocolate topping in a microwave-safe container for 20 to 30 seconds, or until it is easy to pour. Drizzle the topping over the cake. Use the back of a spoon to spread it evenly. Allow the topping to cool if it is warm.

FROST the cake with the whipped topping. Garnish with fresh raspberries and chocolate shavings.

STORE covered in the refrigerator.

devoted to chocolate poke cake

You can't go wrong when you pile on the chocolate! This poke cake starts with a chocolate cake and is filled with a thick, lip-smacking hot fudge sauce, then topped with a light chocolate mousse, brownie pieces and chocolate chips.

PREP TIME: 10 MINUTES + CHILLING
COOK TIME: 35 MINUTES
YIELD: 18–24 SERVINGS

1 (15.25-oz [432-g]) box chocolate cake mix

1 (11.5–15.5-oz [326–439-g]) jar hot fudge sauce

1 (3.4-oz [96-g]) package chocolate instant pudding mix

2 cups (475 ml) cold milk

2 cups (150 g) frozen whipped topping

1 cup (135 g) chopped brownies

½ cup (84 g) chocolate chips

PREPARE and bake the cake according to package directions, using a 13 x 9-inch (33 x 23-cm) cake pan. Let the cake cool for 15 to 20 minutes. Using the round end of a wooden spoon, poke holes in the cake every ½ inch (1.3 cm) to 1 inch (2.5 cm).

MICROWAVE the hot fudge sauce for 20 to 30 seconds, or until it is easy to pour. Evenly pour over the poked cake, filling the holes as much as possible. Place the covered cake in the refrigerator for 2 to 4 hours or until the hot fudge sauce is set.

COMBINE the pudding mix and milk in a large bowl with a whisk until well combined. Fold in the whipped topping. Evenly spread the pudding mixture over the top of the cake using the back of a spoon or an offset spatula. Refrigerate for at least 2 hours before serving.

JUST before serving, evenly sprinkle the brownies and chocolate chips over the top.

STORE covered in the refrigerator.

cherry bomb poke cake

Imagine a chocolate and cherry explosion in your mouth—that's a Cherry Bomb Poke Cake! Starting with a chocolate cake, add cherry gelatin and cherry pie filling, then top it all off with a quick chocolate icing.

PREP TIME: 10 MINUTES + CHILLING
COOK TIME: 35 MINUTES
YIELD: 18–24 SERVINGS

1 (15.25-oz [432-g]) box chocolate cake mix

1 (3-oz [85-g]) package cherry gelatin mix

1 cup (240 ml) boiling water

1 cup (240 ml) cold water

1 (21-oz [595-g]) can cherry pie filling

1 (16-oz [453-g]) can chocolate frosting

Reddi-wip Dairy Whipped Topping, for garnish

Maraschino cherries with stems, for garnish

PREPARE and bake the cake according to package directions, using a 13 x 9-inch (33 x 23-cm) cake pan. Let the cake cool for 15 to 20 minutes. Using a wooden skewer, poke holes all over the cake; make plenty of holes so the filling can soak into the cake.

MIX the gelatin with the boiling water until dissolved. Whisk in the cold water until the gelatin starts to thicken. Pour the gelatin evenly over the cake, filling the holes as much as possible. Place the cherry pie filling in the bowl of a food processor. Cover and pulse a few times until the cherries are in very small pieces. Evenly spread the cherry pie filling over the top of the cake.

MICROWAVE the chocolate frosting in a microwave-safe container for 15 to 20 seconds, or until it is easy to pour. Drizzle the melted frosting over the cake. Use the back of a spoon or an offset spatula to spread it evenly. Refrigerate for at least 2 hours before serving.

JUST before serving, garnish with a dollop of whipped topping and a maraschino cherry.

STORE covered in the refrigerator.

SIMPLE FRUIT POKE CAKES TO TEASE YOUR TASTE BUDS

Life's sweeter with a little cake.

Hold on to your forks—you're going to love the flavor combos in this chapter! With Raspberry Zinger Poke Cake (page 73), Put the Lime in the Coconut Poke Cake (page 89), Strawberry Blast Poke Cake (page 78) or Peach Melba Poke Cake (page 85), prepare to give your taste buds a flavor explosion!

cream of coconut poke cake

If you love coconut, then you will adore this Coconut Cream Poke Cake! It is full of coconut flavor and it is so moist. It's perfect for potlucks and summer picnics.

PREP TIME: 10 MINUTES + CHILLING
COOK TIME: 35 MINUTES
YIELD: 18-24 SERVINGS

1 (15.25-oz [432-g]) box white cake mix

3 large eggs

1 cup (240 ml) milk

½ cup (120 ml) vegetable oil

1 (3.4-oz [96-g]) package coconut cream instant pudding

1 tsp vanilla

1 (15-oz [425-g]) can cream of coconut

1 (14-oz [397-g]) can sweetened condensed milk

1 (8-oz [227-g]) tub frozen whipped topping, thawed

Sweetened coconut flakes

PREHEAT the oven to 350°F (177°C). Spray a 13 x 9-inch (33 x 23-cm) cake pan with cooking spray.

MIX together the cake mix, eggs, milk, oil, instant pudding and vanilla until smooth. Pour into the prepared pan. Bake at for 32 to 35 minutes or until a toothpick inserted near the center of the cake comes out clean.

MIX the cream of coconut and sweetened condensed milk in a medium bowl. Using the round end of a wooden spoon, poke holes in the cake every ½ inch (1.3 cm) to 1 inch (2.5 cm). Slowly pour the coconut mixture over the cake, filling the holes as much as possible. Let the cake cool completely.

TOP with the whipped topping and sprinkle with the desired amount of sweetened coconut flakes.

REFRIGERATE for at least 8 hours before serving. It's even better the next day (if you can wait that long!).

STORE covered in the refrigerator.

piña colada poke cake

Feel like you're on island time with this Piña Colada Poke Cake. This heavenly poke cake is filled with pineapple, coconut and rum.

PREP TIME: 10 MINUTES + CHILLING
COOK TIME: 35 MINUTES
YIELD: 18–24 SERVINGS

1 (20-oz [567-g]) can crushed pineapple

1 (18.25-oz [517-g]) box Duncan Hines Moist Deluxe Pineapple Supreme cake mix

1 (3.4-oz [96-g]) package coconut cream instant pudding mix

1¾ cups (420 ml) milk

¼ cup (60 ml) rum

1 (8-oz [227-g]) tub frozen whipped topping, thawed

1 tsp rum extract

1 (7-oz [198-g]) bag shredded sweetened coconut flakes

EMPTY the pineapple into a colander or strainer and allow it to drain while preparing and baking the cake.

BAKE the cake according to package directions using a 13 x 9-inch (33 x 23-cm) cake pan. Let the cake cool for 15 to 20 minutes. Using the round end of a wooden spoon, poke holes in the cake every ½ inch (1.3 cm) to 1 inch (2.5 cm).

MIX the pudding mix with the milk and rum in a medium bowl. Slowly pour the pudding mixture over the cake, filling the holes as much as possible. Let the cake cool completely.

SPREAD the drained pineapple evenly over the cooled cake. Gently mix the whipped topping and rum extract. Evenly cover the cake with the whipped topping. Sprinkle the coconut evenly over the top. Refrigerate for at least 4 hours before serving.

STORE covered in the refrigerator.

NOTE: To make this nonalcoholic, substitute additional milk for the rum.

raspberry zinger poke cake

If you loved those tasty raspberry and coconut snack cakes as a kid, you're going to love this poke cake version!

PREP TIME: 10 MINUTES + CHILLING
COOK TIME: 35 MINUTES
YIELD: 18–24 SERVINGS

1 (15.25-oz [432-g]) box white cake mix

1 (3-oz [85-g]) package raspberry gelatin mix

1 cup (240 ml) boiling water

1 cup (240 ml) cold water

1 (10-oz [284-g]) jar raspberry preserves

1 (8-oz [227-g]) tub frozen whipped topping, thawed

1 (7-oz [198-g]) bag shredded coconut

PREPARE and bake the cake according to package directions, using a 13 x 9-inch (33 x 23-cm) cake pan. Let the cake cool for 15 to 20 minutes. Using a wooden skewer, poke holes all over the cake; make plenty of holes so the filling can soak into the cake.

MIX the gelatin with the boiling water until dissolved. Whisk in the cold water until the gelatin starts to thicken. Pour the gelatin evenly over the cake, filling the holes as much as possible.

MICROWAVE the raspberry preserves in a small bowl with the lid off until easy to spread, about 30 seconds. Pour the preserves over the top of the cake and spread evenly. Top with whipped topping. Sprinkle the shredded coconut over the top. Refrigerate for at least 4 hours before serving.

STORE covered in the refrigerator.

lemon lover's poke cake

This cake reminds me of a sunny day. Its bright flavors and the burst of lemon make it one of my faves!

PREP TIME: 10 MINUTES + CHILLING
COOK TIME: 35 MINUTES
YIELD: 18–24 SERVINGS

1 (15.25-oz [432-g]) box lemon cake mix

2 (3.4-oz [96-g]) packages lemon instant pudding mix, divided

4 cups (950 ml) cold milk, divided

1 (10-oz [284-g]) jar lemon curd

1 (8-oz [227-g]) tub frozen whipped topping, thawed

Lemon slices, for garnish

Mint leaves, for garnish

PREPARE and bake the cake according to package directions, using a 13 x 9-inch (33 x 23-cm) cake pan. Let the cake cool for 15 to 20 minutes. Using the round end of a wooden spoon, poke holes in the cake every ½ inch (1.3 cm) to 1 inch (2.5 cm).

EMPTY one of the packages of pudding mix into a medium-sized bowl and add 2 cups (475 ml) of milk. Whisk briskly for 2 minutes or until the pudding is dissolved. Evenly pour over the poked cake, filling the holes as much as possible. Evenly spread the lemon curd over the top. Place the covered cake in the refrigerator for 2 to 4 hours or until the pudding is set.

COMBINE the second package of pudding mix with the additional 2 cups (475 ml) of milk in a medium bowl. Carefully fold in the whipped topping. Spread the mixture evenly over the top of the cake.

GARNISH with lemon slices and mint leaves just before serving.

STORE covered in the refrigerator.

watergate poke cake

If you're familiar with Watergate salad, then you know the idea behind this cake. This is a pistachio cake with mandarin oranges, topped with pistachio pudding, crushed pineapple, coconut and pecans!

PREP TIME: 10 MINUTES + CHILLING
COOK TIME: 35-40 MINUTES
YIELD: 18-24 SERVINGS

1 (15.25-oz [432-g]) box white cake mix

2 (3.4-oz [96-g]) packages pistachio instant pudding mix, divided

2 large eggs

1½ (350 ml) cups water

½ cup (60 g) sour cream

¼ cup (63 ml) vegetable oil

5 drops green food coloring, optional

2 (4-oz [114-g]) snack cups Mandarin oranges, drained and chopped

2 cups (475 ml) cold milk

1 (20-oz [567-g]) can crushed pineapple, drained

1 (8-oz [227-g]) tub frozen whipped topping, thawed

1 cup (85 g) shredded coconut

½ cup (55 g) chopped pecans

PREHEAT the oven to 350°F (177°C). Lightly spray a 13 x 9-inch (33 x 23-cm) cake pan with cooking spray and set aside.

COMBINE the cake mix, one package of pistachio pudding mix, eggs, water, sour cream, vegetable oil and food coloring (if using) in a large mixing bowl. Stir in the Mandarin oranges. Spread the mixture into the prepared pan and bake for 35 to 40 minutes or until a toothpick inserted near the center of the cake comes out clean. Let the cake cool for 15 to 20 minutes. Using the round end of a wooden spoon, poke holes in the cake every ½ inch (1.3 cm) to 1 inch (2.5 cm).

EMPTY the second package of pudding mix into a medium-sized bowl and add the milk. Whisk briskly for 2 minutes or until the pudding is dissolved. Evenly pour over the poked cake, filling the holes as much as possible. Place covered cake in the refrigerator for 2 to 4 hours or until the pudding is set.

SPREAD the whipped topping evenly over the cake. Just before serving, sprinkle the coconut and pecans over the top.

STORE covered in the refrigerator.

strawberry blast poke cake

This is the perfect cake for a girl's birthday party or baby shower...or for anyone who loves strawberries!

PREP TIME: 10 MINUTES + CHILLING
COOK TIME: 35 MINUTES
YIELD: 18–24 SERVINGS

1 (15.25-oz [432-g]) box strawberry cake mix

2 (3-oz [85-g]) packages strawberry gelatin mix, divided

2⅔ cups (630 ml) hot water, divided

1 (18-oz [510-g]) jar strawberry preserves

4 ice cubes

1 (8-oz [227-g]) tub frozen whipped topping, thawed

1 cup (340 g) fresh strawberries, diced

Fresh strawberries, for garnish

PREPARE and bake the cake according to package directions, using a 13 x 9-inch (33 x 23-cm) cake pan. Let the cake cool for 15 to 20 minutes. Using a wooden skewer, poke holes all over the cake; make plenty of holes so the filling can soak into the cake.

EMPTY one package of gelatin into a medium-sized bowl with 2 cups (475 ml) of hot water and stir until dissolved. Pour the mixture evenly over the cake, filling the holes as much as you can. Microwave the strawberry preserves in a microwave-safe container for 30 to 45 seconds or until it pours easily. Pour the preserves evenly over the cake. Let the cake cool completely.

COMBINE the second package of gelatin with ⅔ cup (160 ml) hot water in a large bowl, stirring until the gelatin is fully dissolved. Add the ice and stir until the gelatin starts to thicken. Whisk in the whipped topping. Stir in the diced strawberries. Evenly spread the mixture over the cake. Refrigerate for 4 hours or until set. Just before serving, garnish with strawberries.

STORE covered in the refrigerator.

strawberry lemonade poke cake

Strawberries and lemons make the perfect pair in this Strawberry Lemonade Poke Cake.

PREP TIME: 10 MINUTES + CHILLING
COOK TIME: 35 MINUTES
YIELD: 18-24 SERVINGS

1 (15.25-oz [432-g]) box yellow cake mix

1 cup (240 ml) prepared lemonade

½ cup (120 ml) vegetable oil

3 large eggs

1 (14-oz [397-g]) can sweetened condensed milk

1 (10-oz [284-g]) jar lemon curd

1 (21-oz [595-g]) can strawberry pie filling

1 (8-oz [227-g]) tub frozen whipped topping, thawed

Fresh strawberry and lemon slices, for garnish

PREHEAT the oven to 350°F (177°C). Lightly spray a 13 x 9-inch (33 x 23-cm) cake pan with cooking spray and set aside.

MIX the cake mix, lemonade, vegetable oil and eggs in a large mixing bowl until well combined. Spread the mixture into the prepared pan and bake for 30 to 35 minutes or until a toothpick inserted near the center of the cake comes out clean. Let the cake cool for 15 to 20 minutes. Using the round end of a wooden spoon, poke holes in the cake every ½ inch (1.3 cm) to 1 inch (2.5 cm).

COMBINE the sweetened condensed milk and lemon curd in a medium bowl. Whisk briskly to combine. Evenly pour over the poked cake, filling the holes as much as possible. Evenly spread the strawberry pie filling over the top. Spread the whipped topping evenly over the pie filling. Refrigerate for at least 4 hours. Just before serving, garnish with fresh strawberry and lemon slices.

STORE covered in the refrigerator.

caramel apple spice poke pake

This cake is so perfect for fall! A mildly spiced cake is studded with apples and then topped with ooey gooey caramel and toffee bits.

PREP TIME: 10 MINUTES + CHILLING
COOK TIME: 35 MINUTES
YIELD: 18–24 SERVINGS

1 (15.25-oz [432-g]) box white cake mix

2 tsp (5 g) apple pie spice

1 (21-oz [595-g]) can apple pie filling, coarsely chopped

1 (11-oz [312-g]) jar caramel topping

1 (8-oz [227-g]) tub frozen whipped topping, thawed

1 cup (156 g) toffee bits

Additional caramel sauce, for drizzling

PREHEAT the oven to 350°F (177°C). Lightly spray a 13 x 9-inch (33 x 23-cm) cake pan with cooking spray and set aside.

PREPARE the cake according to package directions, adding the apple pie spice and mixing until well combined. Fold in the pie filling. Spread the mixture into the prepared pan and bake for 30 to 35 minutes or until a toothpick inserted near the center of the cake comes out clean. Let the cake cool for 15 to 20 minutes. Using the round end of a wooden spoon, poke holes in the cake every ½ inch (1.3 cm) to 1 inch (2.5 cm).

MICROWAVE the caramel topping, with the lid off, for about 45 seconds or until it pours easily. Pour the caramel evenly over the cake, filling the holes as much as possible. Let the cake cool completely.

SPREAD the whipped topping evenly over the cake. Sprinkle with toffee bits. Drizzle with additional caramel sauce.

STORE covered in the refrigerator.

peach melba poke cake

If you're a fan of peaches and raspberries together, then this is the cake for you! Flavored with vanilla, peaches and raspberries, this cake is perfect for any occasion.

PREP TIME: 10 MINUTES + CHILLING
COOK TIME: 35 MINUTES
YIELD: 18–24 SERVINGS

1 (15.25-oz [432-g]) box white cake mix

2 (3-oz [85-g]) packages peach gelatin mix, divided

3½ cups (825 ml) boiling water, divided

1 (18-oz [510-g]) jar seedless raspberry jam

1 (14-oz [397-g]) can sweetened condensed milk

1 (8-oz [227-g]) tub frozen whipped topping, thawed

Fresh peach slices, for garnish

Fresh raspberries, for garnish

Fresh mint leaves, for garnish

PREPARE and bake the cake according to package directions, using a 13 x 9-inch (33 x 23-cm) cake pan. Let the cake cool for 15 to 20 minutes. Using the round end of a wooden spoon, poke holes in the cake every ½ inch (1.3 cm) to 1 inch (2.5 cm).

EMPTY one package of gelatin into a medium-sized bowl and add 2 cups (475 ml) boiling water. Whisk briskly for 2 minutes or until the gelatin is dissolved. Evenly pour over the poked cake, filling the holes as much as possible. In a separate large bowl, break up the jam until it is mostly smooth. Add the can of sweetened condensed milk and mix until well combined. Pour the sweetened condensed milk mixture evenly over the top of the cake. Place the covered cake in the refrigerator for 2 to 4 hours or until the gelatin is set.

PLACE the second package of gelatin in a large bowl and add 1½ cups (350 ml) boiling water. Stir until completely dissolved. Whisk in the whipped topping until blended. Refrigerate the mixture at least 2 hours.

SPREAD the whipped topping mixture over the cake. Refrigerate for at least 4 hours. Just before serving, garnish the cake with fresh peach slices, fresh raspberries and mint leaves.

STORE covered in the refrigerator.

summer breeze poke cake

This cake reminds me of sitting on the front porch swing soaking up the warm sunshine and feeling a gentle summer breeze. Let this lemon cake, poked with white chocolate pudding then topped with blueberries and a lemony mousse, transport you to a place where there isn't a care in the world!

PREP TIME: 10 MINUTES + CHILLING
COOK TIME: 35 MINUTES
YIELD: 18–24 SERVINGS

1 (15.25-oz [432-g]) box lemon cake mix

1 (3.4-oz [96-g]) package white chocolate instant pudding mix

4 cups (950 ml) cold milk, divided

1 (21-oz [595-g]) can blueberry pie filling

1 (3.4-oz [96-g]) package lemon instant pudding mix

1 (8-oz [227-g]) tub frozen whipped topping, thawed

Fresh blueberries, for garnish

Fresh lemon slices, for garnish

Fresh mint leaves, for garnish

PREPARE and bake the cake according to package directions, using a 13 x 9-inch (33 x 23-cm) cake pan. Let the cake cool for 15 to 20 minutes. Using the round end of a wooden spoon, poke holes in the cake every ½ inch (1.3 cm) to 1 inch (2.5 cm).

EMPTY the white chocolate pudding mix into a medium-sized bowl and add 2 cups (475 ml) of milk. Whisk briskly for 2 minutes or until the pudding is dissolved. Evenly pour over the poked cake, filling the holes as much as possible. Evenly spread the pie filling over the top.

COMBINE the lemon pudding mix with the remaining 2 cups (475 ml) of milk in a large bowl. Whisk briskly for 2 minutes or until the pudding is dissolved. Whisk in the whipped topping. Evenly spread the whipped topping mixture over the cake. Refrigerate for at least 4 hours. Just before serving, garnish with fresh blueberries, lemon slices and mint leaves.

STORE covered in the refrigerator.

put the lime in the coconut poke cake

You know the song, now you can have the cake! This recipe starts with a coconut cake that is poked with a sweet lime mixture and then topped off with even more coconut goodness.

PREP TIME: 10 MINUTES + CHILLING
COOK TIME: 35 MINUTES
YIELD: 18–24 SERVINGS

1 (15.25-oz [432-g]) box white cake mix

3 large eggs

3 cups (715 ml) milk, divided

½ cup (120 ml) vegetable oil

2 (3.4-oz [96-g]) packages coconut cream instant pudding mix, divided

1 tsp vanilla extract

1 (14-oz [397-g]) can sweetened condensed milk

2 (10-oz [284-g]) jars lime curd

1 (8-oz [227-g]) tub frozen whipped topping, thawed

1 cup (85 g) sweetened coconut flakes

Fresh lime slices, for garnish

PREHEAT the oven to 350°F (177°C). Spray a 13 x 9-inch (33 x 23-cm) cake pan with cooking spray and set aside.

MIX together the cake mix, eggs, 1 cup (240 ml) of milk, oil, one package of instant pudding and vanilla extract until smooth. Pour into a prepared pan. Bake for 32 to 35 minutes or until a toothpick inserted near the center of the cake comes out clean. Let the cake cool for 15 to 20 minutes. Using the round end of a wooden spoon, poke holes in the cake every ½ inch (1.3 cm) to 1 inch (2.5 cm).

COMBINE the sweetened condensed milk with the lime curd in a large bowl. Whisk until well combined. Pour the mixture evenly over the cake, filling the holes as much as possible. Let the cake cool completely.

EMPTY the second package of pudding mix into a medium-sized bowl and add the remaining 2 cups (475 ml) of milk. Whisk briskly for 2 minutes or until the pudding is dissolved. Whisk in the whipped topping. Evenly spread the whipped topping mixture over the cake. Sprinkle with coconut flakes. Place the covered cake in the refrigerator for 2 to 4 hours or until the pudding is set. Just before serving, garnish with lime slices.

STORE covered in the refrigerator.

strawberry lemon shortcake poke cake

One of my favorite summer treats is strawberry shortcake. A few years ago, I decided to kick my beloved dessert up a notch with the addition of a lemon cream sauce. Now, it's my favorite way to eat it!

PREP TIME: 10 MINUTES + CHILLING
COOK TIME: 35 MINUTES
YIELD: 18–24 SERVINGS

1 (16-oz [484-g]) package fresh strawberries, hulled and sliced

Juice of 1 lemon

¼ cup (50 g) granulated sugar

1 (15.25-oz [432-g]) box yellow cake mix

1 (3-oz [85-g]) package strawberry gelatin mix

2 cups (475 ml) boiling water

1 (10-oz [284-g]) jar lemon curd

1 (8-oz [227-g]) tub frozen whipped topping, thawed

Fresh strawberries, for garnish

COMBINE the strawberries, lemon juice and sugar in a medium bowl. Mix well and set aside.

PREPARE and bake the cake according to package directions, using a 13 x 9-inch (33 x 23-cm) cake pan. Let the cake cool for 15 to 20 minutes. Using a wooden skewer, poke holes all over the cake; make plenty of holes so the filling can soak into the cake.

EMPTY the gelatin package into a medium-sized bowl and add the water. Whisk briskly for 2 minutes or until the gelatin is dissolved. Evenly pour over the poked cake, filling the holes as much as possible. In a separate medium bowl, combine the strawberries with the lemon curd. Evenly spread the strawberry-lemon curd mixture over the cake. Let the cake cool completely.

SPREAD the whipped topping evenly over the cake. Place the covered cake in the refrigerator for 4 hours. Just before serving, garnish with fresh strawberries.

STORE covered in the refrigerator.

EASY AS A-B-C KID-FRIENDLY POKE CAKES

These fun poke cakes will help you remember the good ol' days!

Although the title implies this chapter is just for kids, let me clarify that it's also for those of us who are kids at heart. If you're a fan of PB&J, I've got a cake for you (page 97). Can't get enough of Cookies & Cream? I've got you covered with a fun and easy poke cake full of both (page 98). Do you think sprinkles are for winners? Then you have to try the Funfetti Poke Cake (page 113) because nothing says, "I love sprinkles," quite like funfetti! Do you secretly love Butterbeer? Make sure you try it as a poke cake (page 106).

cookies & cream poke cake

Boxed chocolate cake mix gets a yummy flavor boost with the addition of chocolate sandwich cookies in this delicious recipe!

PREP TIME: 10 MINUTES + CHILLING
COOK TIME: 35 MINUTES
YIELD: 18-24 SERVINGS

1 (15.25-oz [432-g]) box chocolate cake mix

1 (14-oz [397-g]) can sweetened condensed milk

1 (4.2-oz [119-g]) package cookies & cream instant pudding mix

2 cups (475 ml) cold milk

1 (8-oz [227-g]) tub frozen whipped topping, thawed

20–25 chocolate sandwich cookies, coarsely chopped

PREPARE and bake the cake according to package directions, using a 13 x 9-inch (33 x 23-cm) cake pan. Let the cake cool for 15 to 20 minutes. Using the round end of a wooden spoon, poke holes in the cake every ½ inch (1.3 cm) to 1 inch (2.5 cm).

POUR the sweetened condensed milk over the top of the cake, filling the holes as much as possible. Empty the pudding mix into a medium-sized bowl and add the milk. Whisk briskly for 2 minutes or until the pudding is dissolved. Evenly pour over the poked cake, filling the holes as much as possible. Let the cake cool completely.

EVENLY spread the whipped topping over the cake. Sprinkle with the cookies. Refrigerate for at least 4 hours before serving.

STORE covered in the refrigerator.

banana split poke cake

You have to try a banana split in a poke cake
...it just might be your new favorite thing!

PREP TIME: 10 MINUTES + CHILLING
COOK TIME: 35 MINUTES
YIELD: 18–24 SERVINGS

1 (15.25-oz [432-g]) box white cake mix

1 (3.4-oz [96-g]) package banana instant pudding mix

2 cups (475 ml) cold milk

1 cup (240 ml) strawberry ice cream topping

1 cup (240 ml) pineapple ice cream topping

1 (8-oz [227-g]) tub frozen whipped topping, thawed

¼ cup (60 ml) chocolate sauce

¼ cup (37 g) chopped peanuts

¼ cup (45 g) colored sprinkles

Maraschino cherries

PREPARE and bake the cake according to package directions, using a 13 x 9-inch (33 x 23-cm) cake pan. Let the cake cool for 15 to 20 minutes. Using the round end of a wooden spoon, poke holes in the cake every ½ inch (1.3 cm) to 1 inch (2.5 cm).

EMPTY the pudding mix into a medium-sized bowl and add the milk. Whisk briskly for 2 minutes or until the pudding is dissolved. Evenly pour over the poked cake, filling the holes as much as possible. Spoon dollops of strawberry ice cream topping and pineapple ice cream topping over the cake. Use the back of a spoon to even out and swirl the toppings together. Let the cake cool completely.

SPREAD the whipped topping over the cake. Drizzle chocolate sauce over the topping. Sprinkle with chopped peanuts and sprinkles. Garnish with cherries. Refrigerate for at least 4 hours before serving.

STORE covered in the refrigerator.

root beer float poke cake

A childhood favorite turned into a poke cake! You won't believe how easy it is to turn a box of cake mix into a tempting and fun Root Beer Float Poke Cake.

PREP TIME: 10 MINUTES + CHILLING
COOK TIME: 32-36 MINUTES
YIELD: 18-24 SERVINGS

1 (15.25-oz [432-g]) box white cake mix

1¼ cups (300 ml) root beer

¼ cup (60 ml) vegetable oil

2 large eggs

1 (3.4-oz [96-g]) package vanilla instant pudding mix

2 cups (475 ml) cold milk

2 tsp (10 ml) root beer concentrate

1 (8-oz [227-g]) tub frozen whipped topping, thawed

⅓ cup (73 g) crushed root beer–flavored hard candies (about 10)

PREHEAT the oven to 350°F (177°C). Lightly spray a 13 x 9-inch (33 x 23-cm) cake pan with cooking spray and set aside.

BEAT together the cake mix, root beer, vegetable oil and eggs in a large bowl until well combined. Pour into a prepared pan. Bake for 32 to 36 minutes or until a toothpick inserted near the center of the cake comes out clean. Let the cake cool for 15 to 20 minutes. Using the round end of a wooden spoon, poke holes in the cake every ½ inch (1.3 cm) to 1 inch (2.5 cm).

EMPTY the pudding mix into a medium-sized bowl and add the milk and root beer concentrate. Whisk briskly for 2 minutes or until the pudding is dissolved. Evenly pour over the poked cake, filling the holes as much as possible. Allow the cake to cool completely.

EVENLY spread the whipped topping over the top of the cake. Sprinkle with crushed candies. Refrigerate for at least 4 hours before serving.

STORE covered in the refrigerator.

fluffernutter poke cake

Mmmmm, peanut butter and marshmallow creme. You know it's amazing on a sandwich, but it's even better when it's made into a poke cake.

PREP TIME: 10 MINUTES + CHILLING
COOK TIME: 35 MINUTES
YIELD: 18-24 SERVINGS

1 (15.25-oz [432-g]) box golden butter cake mix

1 cup (180 g) creamy peanut butter, divided

½ cup (1 stick [113 g]) butter, softened

4 eggs

⅔ cup (160 ml) water

1 (3.4-oz [96-g]) package vanilla instant pudding mix

2 cups + 5 tbsp (550 ml) cold milk, divided

1 (13-oz [369-g]) jar marshmallow creme

1 (8-oz [227-g]) tub frozen whipped topping, thawed

½ cup (21 g) Mallow Bits

PREHEAT the oven to 350°F (177°C). Spray the bottom of a 13 x 9-inch (33 x 23-cm) cake pan with cooking spray and set aside.

COMBINE the cake mix, ½ cup (90 g) peanut butter, butter, eggs and water in a large bowl with an electric hand mixer until smooth, about 2 to 3 minutes.

POUR the batter into a prepared cake pan. Bake for 27 to 35 minutes or until a toothpick inserted near the center of the cake comes out clean. Let the cake cool for 15 to 20 minutes. Using the round end of a wooden spoon, poke holes in the cake every ½ inch (1.3 cm) to 1 inch (2.5 cm).

EMPTY the pudding mix into a medium-sized bowl and add 2 cups (475 ml) of milk. Whisk briskly for 2 minutes or until the pudding is dissolved. Whisk in the marshmallow creme. Evenly pour the marshmallow mixture over the poked cake, filling the holes as much as possible. Let the cake cool completely.

WHISK together ¼ cup (45 g) peanut butter and whipped topping in a large bowl. Evenly spread the mixture over the cake.

COMBINE ¼ cup (45 g) creamy peanut butter and 5 tablespoons (75 ml) milk in a small microwave-safe bowl. Microwave in 10-second intervals until smooth, stirring between each time. Carefully pour the mixture into a small zip-top bag and snip a small piece off one of the bottom corners. Squeeze the bag to drizzle the peanut butter glaze over the top of the cake. Sprinkle with Mallow Bits. Refrigerate for at least 4 hours before serving.

STORE covered in the refrigerator.

butterbeer poke cake

Any kid who loves the Harry Potter books by J. K. Rowling will enjoy this Butterbeer Poke Cake. A yellow cake mix is infused with butterbeer flavors—cream soda, butterscotch and caramel. No magic skills needed for this recipe.

PREP TIME: 10 MINUTES + CHILLING
COOK TIME: 35 MINUTES
YIELD: 18-24 SERVINGS

1 (15.25-oz [432-g]) box yellow cake mix

3 large eggs

½ cup (120 ml) vegetable oil

1 cup (240 ml) cream soda

2 (3.4-oz [96-g]) packages butterscotch instant pudding mix, divided

2 cups (475 ml) cold milk

1¼ cups (300 ml) caramel topping, divided

1 (8-oz [227-g]) tub frozen whipped topping, thawed

PREHEAT the oven to 350°F (177°C). Spray the bottom of a 13 x 9-inch (33 x 23-cm) cake pan with cooking spray and set aside.

COMBINE the cake mix, eggs, oil, soda and one box of pudding mix in a large bowl with an electric hand mixer until smooth, about 2 to 3 minutes.

POUR the batter into a prepared cake pan. Bake for 27 to 35 minutes or until a toothpick inserted near the center of the cake comes out clean. Let the cake cool for 15 to 20 minutes. Using the round end of a wooden spoon, poke holes in the cake every ½ inch (1.3 cm) to 1 inch (2.5 cm).

EMPTY the remaining package of pudding mix into a medium-sized bowl and add the milk. Whisk briskly for 2 minutes or until the pudding is dissolved. Evenly pour over the poked cake, filling the holes as much as possible. Pour 1 cup (240 ml) of caramel sauce over the top. Let the cake cool completely.

SPREAD the whipped topping evenly over the caramel sauce. Drizzle the remaining ¼ cup (60 ml) of caramel topping over the whipped topping. Refrigerate for at least 4 hours before serving.

STORE covered in the refrigerator.

watermelon poke cake

One of my favorite things about summer is the arrival of all of the fresh produce. I look forward to watermelon season all year long and one day I realized I could capture the essence of summer with this Watermelon Poke Cake. Not only is this cake watermelon flavored, but it also mimics the colors with its bright pink cake, white rim and green rind.

PREP TIME: 10 MINUTES + CHILLING
COOK TIME: 35 MINUTES
YIELD: 18–24 SERVINGS

1 (15.25-oz [432-g]) box white cake mix

2 (3-oz [85-g]) packages watermelon gelatin mix, divided

1¼ cups (300 ml) lukewarm water

2 large eggs

¼ cup (60 ml) vegetable oil

2 cups (475 ml) boiling water

2 (16-oz [453-g]) cans vanilla frosting

Green food coloring

PREHEAT the oven to 350°F (177°C). Spray the bottom of a 13 x 9-inch (33 x 23-cm) cake pan with cooking spray and set aside.

COMBINE the cake mix, one box of gelatin, lukewarm water, eggs and oil in a large bowl with an electric hand mixer until smooth, about 2 to 3 minutes.

POUR the batter into prepared cake pan. Bake for 27 to 35 minutes or until a toothpick inserted near the center of the cake comes out clean. Let the cake cool for 15 to 20 minutes. Using a wooden skewer or meat fork, poke holes in the cake every ½ inch (1.3 cm) to 1 inch (2.5 cm).

EMPTY the second package of gelatin into a medium-sized bowl and add the boiling water. Whisk briskly for 2 minutes or until the gelatin is dissolved. Evenly pour over the poked cake, filling the holes as much as possible. Cover and refrigerate for 4 hours.

SPREAD one can of vanilla frosting over the cake. Microwave the second can of vanilla frosting in a microwave-safe container for 15 to 20 seconds or until it is easy to pour. Add green food coloring and stir well to combine. Drizzle the melted frosting over the top of the cake. Use the back of a spoon or an offset spatula to spread it evenly. Refrigerate for at least 4 hours before serving.

STORE covered in the refrigerator.

bubble gum poke cake

As bubble gum is a childhood favorite flavor, I knew I needed to include a cake version. A boxed cake mix is given bubble gum flavor and pink coloring. Then, it's poked with vanilla pudding and topped with whipped topping and, of course, gumballs! Kids (and kids-at-heart) will go crazy for this cake.

PREP TIME: 10 MINUTES + CHILLING
COOK TIME: 35 MINUTES
YIELD: 18–24 SERVINGS

1 (15.25-oz [432-g]) box white cake mix

½ tsp Super Strength Bubble Gum flavoring

Pink food coloring

1 (3.4-oz [96-g]) package vanilla instant pudding mix

2 cups (475 ml) cold milk

1 (8-oz [227-g]) tub frozen whipped topping, thawed

Gumballs

Rainbow nonpareils

PREPARE the cake according to package directions, adding the bubble gum flavoring and food coloring, and bake using a 13 x 9-inch (33 x 23-cm) cake pan. Let the cake cool for 15 to 20 minutes. Using the round end of a wooden spoon, poke holes in the cake every ½ inch (1.3 cm) to 1 inch (2.5 cm).

EMPTY the pudding mix into a medium-sized bowl and add the milk. Whisk briskly for 2 minutes or until the pudding is dissolved. Evenly pour over the poked cake, filling the holes as much as possible. Let the cake cool completely.

SPREAD the whipped topping over the cake. Refrigerate for at least 4 hours before serving.

DECORATE with gumballs and sprinkle with nonpareils just before serving.

STORE covered in the refrigerator.

funfetti poke cake

Because sprinkles are for winners, this cake features a white cake mix with fun and colorful sprinkles, poked with a funfetti pudding mix, topped with whipped topping and more sprinkles.

PREP TIME: 10 MINUTES + CHILLING
COOK TIME: 35 MINUTES
YIELD: 18-24 SERVINGS

1 (15.25-oz [432-g]) box white cake mix

1 cup (180 g) rainbow sprinkles, divided

1 (14-oz [397-g]) can sweetened condensed milk

1 (3.4-oz [96-g]) package vanilla instant pudding mix

2 cups (475 ml) cold milk

1 (8-oz [227-g]) tub frozen whipped topping, thawed

PREPARE and bake the cake according to package directions, adding ⅓ cup (60 g) of rainbow sprinkles, using a 13 x 9-inch (33 x 23-cm) cake pan. Let the cake cool for 15 to 20 minutes. Using the round end of a wooden spoon, poke holes in the cake every ½ inch (1.3 cm) to 1 inch (2.5 cm).

POUR the sweetened condensed milk over the top of the cake. Empty the pudding package into a medium-sized bowl and add the milk. Whisk briskly for 2 minutes or until the pudding is dissolved. Stir in ⅓ cup (60 g) of rainbow sprinkles. Evenly pour the pudding mixture over the poked cake, filling the holes as much as possible. Let the cake cool completely.

SPREAD the whipped topping over the cake. Refrigerate for at least 4 hours. Just before serving, sprinkle the remaining ⅓ cup (60 g) of rainbow sprinkles over the top.

STORE covered in the refrigerator.

creamsicle poke cake

When I was younger, I remember chasing down the ice cream truck with money in hand just to get a Creamsicle. Those few moments of eating that Popsicle were heaven. You can easily re-create those flavors in this Creamsicle Poke Cake—go ahead, take a trip down memory lane!

PREP TIME: 10 MINUTES + CHILLING
COOK TIME: 35 MINUTES
YIELD: 18-24 SERVINGS

1 (15.25-oz [432-g]) box white cake mix

2 (3-oz [85-g]) packages orange gelatin mix, divided

1 cup (240 ml) boiling water

1 cup (240 ml) cold water

1 (3.4-oz [96-g]) package vanilla instant pudding mix

2 cups (475 ml) cold milk

2 tsp (10 ml) vanilla extract

1 (8-oz [227-g]) tub frozen whipped topping, thawed

PREPARE and bake the cake according to package directions, using a 13 x 9-inch (33 x 23-cm) cake pan. Let the cake cool for 15 to 20 minutes. Using a wooden skewer, poke holes in the cake every ½ inch (1.3 cm) to 1 inch (2.5 cm).

EMPTY one package of gelatin into a medium-sized bowl and add the boiling water. Whisk briskly until the gelatin is dissolved. Add the cold water and whisk for 2 minutes or until the gelatin begins to thicken. Evenly pour over the poked cake, filling the holes as much as possible. Place the covered cake in the refrigerator for 2 to 4 hours or until the gelatin is set.

EMPTY the pudding mix into a medium-sized bowl and add the milk. Add the second package of gelatin and the vanilla extract. Whisk briskly for 2 minutes or until the pudding and gelatin are dissolved. Fold in the whipped topping. Spread the whipped topping mixture over the cake. Refrigerate for at least 4 hours before serving.

STORE covered in the refrigerator.

jell-o poke cake

One of the great things about poke cakes is the ability to easily change the flavors. This is a very basic poke cake without many frills—just pick your favorite flavor of gelatin for an easy dessert any time!

PREP TIME: 10 MINUTES + CHILLING
COOK TIME: 35 MINUTES
YIELD: 18–24 SERVINGS

1 (15.25-oz [432-g]) box white cake mix

1 (3-oz [85-g]) package any flavor gelatin mix

1 cup (240 ml) boiling water

1 cup (240 ml) cold water

1 (8-oz [227-g]) tub frozen whipped topping, thawed

PREPARE and bake the cake according to package directions, using a 13 x 9-inch (33 x 23-cm) cake pan. Let the cake cool for 15 to 20 minutes. Using a wooden skewer, poke holes all over the cake; make plenty of holes so the filling can soak into the cake.

MIX the gelatin with the boiling water until dissolved. Whisk in the cold water until the gelatin starts to thicken. Pour the gelatin evenly over the cake, filling the holes as much as you can. Cover and refrigerate for 4 hours.

SPREAD the whipped topping over the cake. Refrigerate for at least 4 hours before serving.

STORE covered in the refrigerator.

cherry limeade poke cake

I'm a big fan of fruity drinks and cherry limeade ranks up near the top for me. Wanting to make this flavor profile into a poke cake, I started with a white cake mix and added lime zest. The cake is poked with cherry gelatin and topped off with whipped topping and garnished with fresh limes and cherries. If you're a fan of cherry limeade too, you will love this Cherry Limeade Poke Cake!

PREP TIME: 10 MINUTES + CHILLING
COOK TIME: 35 MINUTES
YIELD: 18–24 SERVINGS

1 (15.25-oz [432-g]) box white cake mix

1 tbsp + 1 tsp (6 g) lime zest, divided

1 (3-oz [85-g]) package cherry gelatin mix

1 cup (240 ml) boiling water

1 cup (240 ml) cold water

1 (8-oz [227-g]) tub frozen whipped topping, thawed

Lime peel twists, for garnish

Maraschino cherries, for garnish

PREPARE and bake the cake according to package directions, adding 1 tablespoon (6 g) of lime zest to the cake batter, using a 13 x 9-inch (33 x 23-cm) cake pan. Let the cake cool for 15 to 20 minutes. Using a wooden skewer, poke holes in the cake every ½ inch (1.3 cm) to 1 inch (2.5 cm).

EMPTY the gelatin into a medium-sized bowl and add the boiling water. Whisk briskly for 2 minutes or until the gelatin is dissolved. Whisk in the cold water until the gelatin starts to thicken. Evenly pour the gelatin over the poked cake, filling the holes as much as possible. Place the covered cake in the refrigerator for 4 hours.

COMBINE the whipped topping and 1 teaspoon of lime zest in a large bowl. Spread the whipped topping mixture evenly over the cake. Refrigerate for at least 4 hours before serving.

GARNISH with lime peel twists and cherries just before serving.

STORE covered in the refrigerator.

See image on page 94.

cookie monster poke cake

Unleash your inner child with this Cookie Monster Poke Cake. This chocolate cake is filled with cookies & cream pudding, and topped with an easy blue icing. And don't forget the best part—lots and lots of cookies on top!

PREP TIME: 10 MINUTES + CHILLING
COOK TIME: 35 MINUTES
YIELD: 18–24 SERVINGS

1 (15.25-oz [432-g]) box chocolate cake mix

2 (3.4-oz [96-g]) packages cookies & cream instant pudding mix

4 cups (950 ml) cold milk

1 (16-oz [453-g]) can vanilla frosting

Royal blue food coloring

1½ cups (168 g) broken assorted cookies for topping (chocolate chip, Oreo, fudge stripe, peanut butter, etc.)

PREPARE and bake the cake according to package directions, using a 13 x 9-inch (33 x 23-cm) cake pan. Let the cake cool for 15 to 20 minutes. Using the round end of a wooden spoon, poke holes in the cake every ½ inch (1.3 cm) to 1 inch (2.5 cm).

EMPTY the pudding mix into a medium-sized bowl and add the milk. Whisk briskly for 2 minutes or until the pudding is dissolved. Evenly pour over the poked cake, filling the holes as much as possible. Place the covered cake in the refrigerator for 2 to 4 hours or until the pudding is set.

MICROWAVE the vanilla frosting in a microwave-safe container for 15 to 20 seconds, or until it is easy to pour. Carefully mix in enough food coloring to color it blue. Drizzle the melted frosting over the cake. Use the back of a spoon or an offset spatula to spread it evenly. Immediately sprinkle the cookie pieces over the top. Refrigerate for at least 2 hours before serving.

STORE covered in the refrigerator.

movie theater poke cake

All of the goodies you love at the movie theater as a tasty poke cake—movie not included! White cake mix is poked with a sweet soda sauce before being topped with all of your favorite movie theater treats.

PREP TIME: 10 MINUTES + CHILLING
COOK TIME: 35 MINUTES
YIELD: 18–24 SERVINGS

1 (15.25-oz [432-g]) box white cake mix

1 (14-oz [397-g]) can sweetened condensed milk

¼ cup (60 ml) cola

1 (16-oz [453-g]) can vanilla frosting

1 cup (8 g) popped butter-flavored popcorn

1 cup (188 g) assorted movie theater candy

PREPARE and bake the cake according to package directions, using a 13 x 9-inch (33 x 23-cm) cake pan. Let the cake cool for 15 to 20 minutes. Using the round end of a wooden spoon, poke holes in the cake every ½ inch (1.3 cm) to 1 inch (2.5 cm).

COMBINE the sweetened condensed milk and the cola in a medium bowl. Pour the sweetened condensed milk mixture evenly over the cake, filling the holes as much as possible. Place the covered cake in the refrigerator for 2 to 4 hours.

MICROWAVE the vanilla frosting in a microwave-safe container for 15 to 20 seconds, or until it is easy to pour. Drizzle the melted frosting over the top of the cake. Use the back of a spoon or an offset spatula to spread it evenly. Refrigerate for at least 2 hours before serving.

TOP with popped popcorn and assorted movie theater candy just before serving.

STORE covered in the refrigerator.

lucky charms poke cake

Skip the bowl and milk—I just found a new way to eat a favorite breakfast cereal! Crushed Lucky Charms are added to a white cake mix, which is then poked with vanilla pudding. The top has even more cereal for a treat the entire family will love.

PREP TIME: 10 MINUTES + CHILLING
COOK TIME: 35 MINUTES
YIELD: 18–24 SERVINGS

1 (15.25-oz [432-g]) box white cake mix

2½ cups (93 g) crushed Lucky Charms cereal, divided

2 (3.4-oz [96-g]) packages vanilla instant pudding mix

4 cups (950 ml) cold milk

1 (8-oz [227-g]) tub frozen whipped topping, thawed

PREPARE and bake the cake according to package directions, adding 1 cup (37 g) crushed Lucky Charms cereal and using a 13 x 9-inch (33 x 23-cm) cake pan. Let the cake cool for 15 to 20 minutes. Using the round end of a wooden spoon, poke holes in the cake every ½ inch (1.3 cm) to 1 inch (2.5 cm).

EMPTY the pudding mix into a medium-sized bowl and add the milk. Whisk briskly for 2 minutes or until the pudding is dissolved. Evenly pour over the poked cake, filling the holes as much as possible. Place covered cake in the refrigerator for 2 to 4 hours or until the pudding is set.

SPREAD the whipped topping evenly over the top. Sprinkle the 1½ cups (56 g) Lucky Charms cereal over the top. Refrigerate for at least 2 hours before serving.

STORE covered in the refrigerator.

dirt poke cake

What kid doesn't love to play in the dirt? This fun cake starts with a chocolate cake mix and adds chocolate pudding. Crushed cookies make the "dirt" on the cake, with some added gummy worms and bugs for good measure.

PREP TIME: 10 MINUTES + CHILLING
COOK TIME: 35 MINUTES
YIELD: 18-24 SERVINGS

1 (15.25-oz [432-g]) box chocolate cake mix

2 (3.4-oz [96-g]) packages chocolate instant pudding mix

4 cups (950 ml) cold milk

1 (16-oz [453-g]) can chocolate frosting

24 Oreo cookies, crushed

Gummy worms

Bug sprinkles

PREPARE and bake the cake according to package directions, using a 13 x 9-inch (33 x 23-cm) cake pan. Let the cake cool for 15 to 20 minutes. Using the round end of a wooden spoon, poke holes in the cake every ½ inch (1.3 cm) to 1 inch (2.5 cm).

EMPTY the pudding mix into a medium-sized bowl and add the milk. Whisk briskly for 2 minutes or until the pudding is dissolved. Evenly pour over the poked cake, filling the holes as much as possible. Place the covered cake in the refrigerator for 2 to 4 hours or until the pudding is set.

SPREAD the chocolate frosting over the top of the cake. Use the back of a spoon or an offset spatula to spread it evenly. Sprinkle the crushed Oreo cookies over the top. Decorate with gummy worms and bug sprinkles. Refrigerate for at least 2 hours before serving.

STORE covered in the refrigerator.

poppin' rocks poke cake

If you've ever had Pop Rocks candy then you know how awesome this cake will be. It's a little bit funky and a whole lot of fun! A white cake mix gets the flavor treatment with grape and green apple gelatin—and it's all topped off with Pop Rocks candy.

PREP TIME: 10 MINUTES + CHILLING
COOK TIME: 35 MINUTES
YIELD: 18–24 SERVINGS

1 (15.25-oz [432-g]) box white cake mix

1 (3-oz [85-g]) package grape gelatin mix

2 cups (475 ml) boiling water, divided

2 cups (475 ml) cold water, divided

1 (2.79-oz [79-g]) package green apple gelatin mix

1 (16-oz [453-g]) can vanilla frosting

3–4 packages grape Pop Rocks candy

3–4 packages green apple Pop Rocks candy

PREPARE and bake the cake according to package directions, using a 13 x 9-inch (33 x 23-cm) cake pan. Let the cake cool for 15 to 20 minutes. Using a wooden skewer, poke holes all over the cake; make plenty of holes so the filling can soak into the cake.

MIX the grape gelatin with 1 cup (240 ml) boiling water until dissolved. Whisk in 1 cup (240 ml) of cold water until the gelatin starts to thicken. Pour the grape gelatin evenly over the cake, filling the holes as much as possible. Mix the green apple gelatin with 1 cup (240 ml) boiling water until dissolved. Whisk in 1 cup (240 ml) cold water until the gelatin starts to thicken. Pour the green apple gelatin evenly over the cake, filling the holes as much as possible.

MICROWAVE the vanilla frosting in a microwave-safe container for 15 to 20 seconds, or until it is easy to pour. Drizzle the melted frosting over the top of the cake. Use the back of a spoon or an offset spatula to spread it evenly. Sprinkle the Pop Rocks candy over the top. Refrigerate for at least 4 hours before serving.

STORE covered in the refrigerator.

IF YOU CAN DREAM IT, YOU CAN ACHIEVE IT

Making life sweeter one bite at a time.

Many of the recipes in this chapter were just for fun. While coming up with ideas for this book, I went into overdrive and came up with more than 100 flavor combinations. I saved some of the more entertaining names and recipes for this chapter. In this chapter, I have a recipe dedicated to Elvis Presley (page 127), the song "Purple Haze" (page 132) and the drink named after golfer Arnold Palmer (page 135)...along with a few adult-only contributions because it's always 5 o'clock somewhere!

ode to elvis poke cake

Celebrate the King of Rock & Roll with this peanut butter cake poked with banana cream pudding and topped with sliced bananas, whipped topping, peanut butter glaze...and optional crispy bacon. Oh, yes—it's over-the-top and crazy indulgent!

PREP TIME: 10 MINUTES + CHILLING
COOK TIME: 35 MINUTES
YIELD: 18–24 SERVINGS

¾ cup (135 g) creamy peanut butter, divided

½ cup (1 stick [113 g]) butter, softened

4 large eggs

1 (15.25-oz [432-g]) box golden butter cake mix

⅔ cup (160 ml) water, divided

1 (3.4-oz [96-g]) package banana cream instant pudding mix

2 cups + 5 tbsp (550 ml) milk, divided

4–5 bananas, peeled and sliced

1 (8-oz [227-g]) tub frozen whipped topping, thawed

12–16 oz (340–454 g) bacon, cooked, crumbled and drained (optional)

PREHEAT the oven to 325°F (163°C). Spray a 13 x 9-inch (33 x 23-cm) cake pan with cooking spray and set aside.

CREAM ½ cup (90 g) of peanut butter and butter in a large bowl with an electric mixer. Add eggs, one at a time, mixing until just combined. Add half of the cake mix and ⅓ cup (80 ml) of water. Mix until just combined. Add the remaining cake mix and remaining ⅓ cup (80 ml) of water; mix until just combined. Pour the batter evenly into the prepared baking pan. Bake for 30 to 35 minutes or until a toothpick inserted near the center of the cake comes out clean. Remove from the oven, and with the handle end of a wooden spoon, poke holes all over the cake; make plenty of holes so the pudding can soak into the cake.

EMPTY the pudding mix into a medium-sized bowl and add the milk. Whisk briskly for 2 minutes or until the pudding is dissolved. Pour the pudding mixture over the cake, filling the holes as much as possible. Use the back of a spoon to help spread the pudding mix and fill the holes. Top with sliced bananas. Evenly spread the whipped topping over the cake. Sprinkle the crumbled bacon over the top, if using.

COMBINE ¼ cup (45 g) of creamy peanut butter and 5 tablespoons (75 ml) of milk in a small microwave-safe bowl. Microwave in 10-second intervals, stirring between each time, until smooth. Carefully pour the mixture into a small zip-top bag and snip a small piece off one of the bottom corners. Squeeze the bag to drizzle the peanut butter glaze over the top of the cake.

COVER and refrigerate the cake for at least 4 hours before serving.

STORE covered in the refrigerator.

eggnog poke cake

This spiked seasonal cake just might make you wish winter could stay around a little longer. A boxed cake mix is doctored with a subtle hint of eggnog, then poked with a rich and creamy eggnog pudding.

PREP TIME: 10 MINUTES + CHILLING
COOK TIME: 35 MINUTES
YIELD: 18–24 SERVINGS

1 (15.25-oz [432-g]) box white cake mix

3 large eggs

½ cup (120 ml) vegetable oil

2¼ cups (535 ml) eggnog, divided

¾ cup (180 ml) rum, divided

1 (3.4-oz [96-g]) package vanilla instant pudding mix

1 (8-oz [227-g]) tub frozen whipped topping, thawed

Ground nutmeg, for garnish

PREHEAT the oven to 350°F (177°C). Spray a 13 x 9-inch (33 x 23-cm) cake pan with cooking spray and set aside.

COMBINE the cake mix, eggs, vegetable oil, ½ cup (120 ml) of eggnog and ½ cup (120 ml) of rum in a large bowl until thoroughly mixed. Pour the batter evenly into the prepared baking pan. Bake for 25 to 30 minutes or until a toothpick inserted near the center of the cake comes out clean. Remove from the oven, and with the handle of a wooden spoon, poke holes all over the cake; make plenty of holes so the pudding can soak into the cake.

EMPTY the pudding mix into a medium-sized bowl and add the remaining 1¾ cups (415 ml) of eggnog and remaining ¼ cup (60 ml) of rum. Whisk briskly for 2 minutes or until the pudding is dissolved. Evenly pour over the poked cake, filling the holes as much as possible. Spread the whipped topping over the cake. Place the covered cake in the refrigerator for 2 to 4 hours or until the pudding is set.

GARNISH with a sprinkle of ground nutmeg just before serving.

STORE covered in the refrigerator.

NOTE: For a nonalcoholic version, replace all rum listed with extra eggnog.

cape cod spice poke cake

Cranberries and walnuts combine with a boxed spice cake to give you a taste of New England.

PREP TIME: 10 MINUTES + CHILLING
COOK TIME: 35 MINUTES
YIELD: 18–24 SERVINGS

1 (15.25-oz [432-g]) box spice cake mix

1 (3-oz [85-g]) package cranberry gelatin mix

1 cup (240 ml) boiling water

1 cup (240 ml) cold water

1 (14–16-oz [397–453-g]) can whole berry cranberry sauce

½ cup (1 stick [113 g]) butter, softened

8 oz (227 g) cream cheese, softened

1 tsp vanilla extract

4 cups (500 g) powdered sugar

½ cup (55 g) chopped walnuts

PREPARE and bake the cake according to package directions, using a 13 x 9-inch (33 x 23-cm) cake pan. Let the cake cool for 15 to 20 minutes. Using the round end of a wooden spoon, poke holes in the cake every ½ inch (1.3 cm) to 1 inch (2.5 cm).

EMPTY the gelatin package into a medium-sized bowl and add the boiling water. Whisk briskly for 2 minutes or until the gelatin is dissolved. Whisk in the cold water until the gelatin begins to thicken. Add the cranberry sauce and mix well. Evenly pour over the poked cake, filling the holes as much as possible. Place the covered cake in the refrigerator for 2 to 4 hours or until the gelatin is set.

COMBINE the butter, cream cheese, vanilla extract and powdered sugar in a large bowl with an electric mixer until light and fluffy. Spread the cream cheese mixture over the cake. Garnish with walnuts. Refrigerate for at least 4 hours before serving.

STORE covered in the refrigerator.

purple haze poke cake

Purple Haze, all in my brain...and in my poke cake! Inspired by the famous song, this cake is fun for kids' birthdays! A white cake mix is poked with blackberry gelatin, then for an added flavor punch, blackberry jam. To balance out the flavors, a simple buttercream frosting tops the cake and is adorned with an assortment of colorful sprinkles.

PREP TIME: 10 MINUTES + CHILLING
COOK TIME: 35 MINUTES
YIELD: 18–24 SERVINGS

1 (15.25-oz [432-g]) box white cake mix

1 (3-oz [85-g]) package blackberry gelatin mix

1 cup (240 ml) boiling water

1 cup (240 ml) cold water

1½ cups (480 g) blackberry jam

½ cup (1 stick [113 g]) butter, softened

3¾ cups (469 g) powdered sugar

3–4 tbsp (45–60 ml) milk or water

2 tsp (10 ml) vanilla extract

Purple food coloring

¼ cup (45 g) rainbow sprinkles

¼ cup (45 g) rainbow stars confetti sprinkles

PREPARE and bake the cake according to package directions, using a 13 x 9-inch (33 x 23-cm) cake pan. Let the cake cool for 15 to 20 minutes. Using the round end of a wooden spoon, poke holes in the cake every ½ inch (1.3 cm) to 1 inch (2.5 cm).

EMPTY the gelatin package into a medium-sized bowl and add the boiling water. Whisk briskly for 2 minutes or until the gelatin is dissolved. Whisk in the cold water until the gelatin begins to thicken. Whisk in the jam. Evenly pour the jam mixture over the poked cake, filling the holes as much as possible.

BEAT the butter, powdered sugar, milk, vanilla extract and food coloring in a large bowl until well combined. Stir in the rainbow sprinkles and star sprinkles. Evenly spread the frosting over the top of the cake. Refrigerate for at least 4 hours before serving.

STORE covered in the refrigerator.

arnold palmer poke cake

Have you ever had an Arnold Palmer? It's iced tea mixed with lemonade—and it's amazing! This poke cake is a fun and tasty twist on the classic drink.

PREP TIME: 10 MINUTES + CHILLING
COOK TIME: 35 MINUTES
YIELD: 18-24 SERVINGS

2 cups (475 ml) warm milk

4 family-size tea bags, divided

Boiling water (enough to substitute for amount of water listed in the cake mix directions)

1 (15.25-oz [432-g]) box white cake mix

1 (3.4-oz [96-g]) package vanilla instant pudding mix

1 (8-oz [240-g]) package cream cheese

¼ cup (57 g) butter, softened

5 cups (625 g) powdered sugar

3 tbsp (45 ml) fresh lemon juice

1 tbsp (6 g) lemon zest

POUR the warm milk over 2 tea bags and steep for 10 minutes. Squeeze the tea bags into the tea and discard the tea bags. Refrigerate the milk until cold.

POUR the boiling water over the remaining 2 tea bags and steep for 10 minutes. Squeeze the tea bags into the water and discard the tea bags. Allow the water to cool to room temperature.

PREPARE and bake the cake according to package directions, using the tea water in place of the water listed on the box and using a 13 x 9-inch (33 x 23-cm) cake pan. Let the cake cool for 15 to 20 minutes. Using the round end of a wooden spoon, poke holes in the cake every ½ inch (1.3 cm) to 1 inch (2.5 cm).

EMPTY the pudding mix into a medium-sized bowl and add the tea-infused milk. Whisk briskly for 2 minutes or until the pudding is dissolved. Evenly pour over the poked cake, filling the holes as much as possible. Place the covered cake in the refrigerator for 2 to 4 hours or until the pudding is set.

BEAT the cream cheese and butter in a large bowl with an electric mixer until fluffy. Add the powdered sugar, 1 cup (125 g) at a time. Beat well. Add the lemon juice and zest. Evenly spread the frosting over the cake. Refrigerate for at least 4 hours before serving.

STORE covered in the refrigerator.

pistachio poke cake

There is a certain appeal to pistachio desserts—there's something about the nuts and the green pudding that people love. In this recipe, a white cake mix is poked with pistachio pudding and topped with whipped topping along with chopped pistachios.

PREP TIME: 10 MINUTES + CHILLING
COOK TIME: 35 MINUTES
YIELD: 18–24 SERVINGS

1 (15.25-oz [432-g]) box white cake mix

2 (3.4-oz [96-g]) packages pistachio instant pudding mix

4 cups (950 ml) cold milk

1 (8-oz [227-g]) tub frozen whipped topping, thawed

½ cup (55 g) chopped pistachios

PREPARE and bake the cake according to package directions, using a 13 x 9-inch (33 x 23-cm) cake pan. Let the cake cool for 15 to 20 minutes. Using the round end of a wooden spoon, poke holes in the cake every ½ inch (1.3 cm) to 1 inch (2.5 cm).

EMPTY the pudding mix into a medium-sized bowl and add the milk. Whisk briskly for 2 minutes or until the pudding is dissolved. Evenly pour over the poked cake, filling the holes as much as possible. Place the covered cake in the refrigerator for 2 to 4 hours or until the pudding is set.

SPREAD the whipped topping over the cake. Sprinkle with chopped pistachios. Refrigerate for at least 4 hours before serving.

STORE covered in the refrigerator.

pumpkin spice poke cake

This seasonal cake is perfect for fall—it just might be better than pumpkin pie! The spice cake is poked with pumpkin spice pudding and topped off with a creamy whipped topping. Pumpkin candies garnish the cake.

PREP TIME: 10 MINUTES + CHILLING
COOK TIME: 30 MINUTES
YIELD: 18-24 SERVINGS

1 (15.25-oz [432-g]) box spice cake mix

1 (15-oz [425-g]) can 100% pure pumpkin (not pumpkin pie filling)

3 large eggs

2 (3.4-oz [96-g]) packages pumpkin spice instant pudding mix

4 cups (475 ml) milk

1 (8-oz [227-g]) tub whipped topping, thawed

Mellowcreme Pumpkins candies

PREHEAT the oven to 350°F (177°C). Spray a 13 x 9-inch (33 x 23-cm) cake pan with cooking spray and set aside.

BEAT the cake mix, pumpkin and eggs in a large bowl until well combined. Pour the batter into the prepared pan. Bake for 30 minutes or until a toothpick inserted near the center of the cake comes out clean. Let the cake cool for 15 to 20 minutes. Using the round end of a wooden spoon, poke holes in the cake every ½ inch (1.3 cm) to 1 inch (2.5 cm).

EMPTY the pudding mix into a medium-sized bowl and add the milk. Whisk briskly for 2 minutes or until the pudding is dissolved. Evenly pour over the poked cake, filling the holes as much as possible. Place the covered cake in the refrigerator for 2 to 4 hours or until the pudding is set.

SPREAD the whipped topping over the top of the cake. Garnish with Mellowcreme Pumpkins. Refrigerate for at least 4 hours before serving.

STORE covered in the refrigerator.

irish cream poke cake

This is a great cake for St. Patrick's Day—or any time you want an adults-only dessert. This moist cake will knock your socks off!

PREP TIME: 10 MINUTES + CHILLING
COOK TIME: 35 MINUTES
YIELD: 18–24 SERVINGS

1 (15.25-oz [432-g]) box chocolate cake mix

1 tsp mint extract

1 (14-oz [397-g]) can sweetened condensed milk

½ cup (120 ml) Irish cream liqueur

1 (8-oz [227-g]) tub frozen whipped topping, thawed

1 cup (168 g) Andes Creme de Menthe baking chips

PREPARE and bake the cake according to package directions, adding mint extract to the cake mix and using a 13 x 9-inch (33 x 23-cm) cake pan. Let the cake cool for 15 to 20 minutes. Using the round end of a wooden spoon, poke holes in the cake every ½ inch (1.3 cm) to 1 inch (2.5 cm).

WHISK together the sweetened condensed milk and liqueur in a medium bowl. Evenly pour the liqueur mixture over the poked cake, filling the holes as much as possible. Place the covered cake in the refrigerator for 4 hours.

EVENLY spread the whipped topping over the top of the cake. Sprinkle with the baking chips. Refrigerate for at least 4 hours before serving.

STORE covered in the refrigerator.

mudslide poke cake

Take a chocolate cake mix and infuse it with the famous Mudslide cocktail and you have yourself a pretty awesome poke cake. Please eat responsibly!

PREP TIME: 10 MINUTES + CHILLING
COOK TIME: 35 MINUTES
YIELD: 18–24 SERVINGS

1 (15.25-oz [432-g]) box chocolate fudge cake mix

1 (14-oz [397-g]) can sweetened condensed milk

1 (10–12-oz [284–340-g]) jar hot fudge sauce

2 tbsp (30 ml) Bailey's Irish Cream

2 tbsp (30 ml) Kahlua coffee liqueur

2 tbsp (30 ml) vodka

1 (8-oz [227-g]) tub frozen whipped topping, thawed

Chocolate shavings

PREPARE and bake the cake according to package directions, using a 13 x 9-inch (33 x 23-cm) cake pan. Let the cake cool for 15 to 20 minutes. Using the round handle end of a wooden spoon, pokes holes in the cake every 1 inch (2.5 cm) to 1½ inch (3.8 cm).

MIX the sweetened condensed milk, hot fudge sauce, Bailey's Irish Cream, Kahlua and vodka in a medium bowl until smooth. Evenly pour over the poked cake, filling the holes as much as possible. Place the covered cake in the refrigerator for 2 to 4 hours to set.

FROST the cake with whipped topping. Garnish with the chocolate shavings.

STORE covered in the refrigerator.

margarita poke cake

Get the party started with this Margarita Poke Cake! It's great for Mexican-themed parties, girls' nights or any situation that calls for an adult beverage. The lemon cake is flavored with lime zest, margarita mix and alcohol. Poke it with a margarita-tasting pudding mixture and top it off with whipped topping. Salt not required.

PREP TIME: 10 MINUTES + CHILLING
COOK TIME: 35 MINUTES
YIELD: 18–24 SERVINGS

---

1 (15.25-oz [432-g]) box lemon cake mix

Nonalcoholic margarita mix (enough to substitute for amount of water listed in cake mix directions)

4 tbsp (60 ml) tequila, divided

Zest of 1 lime

1 (3.4-oz [96-g]) package lemon instant pudding mix

2 cups (475 ml) cold milk

1 tbsp (15 ml) Triple Sec

Juice of 1 lime

1 (8-oz [227-g]) tub frozen whipped topping, thawed

Lime slices, for garnish

Lime zest, for garnish

PREPARE and bake the cake according to package directions, substituting margarita mix for the water and adding 2 tablespoons (30 ml) of tequila and lime zest to the batter, using a 13 x 9-inch (33 x 23-cm) cake pan. Let the cake cool for 15 to 20 minutes. Using the round end of a wooden spoon, poke holes in the cake every ½ inch (1.3 cm) to 1 inch (2.5 cm).

EMPTY the pudding mix into a medium-sized bowl and add the milk. Whisk briskly for 2 minutes or until the pudding is dissolved. Add 1 tablespoon (15 ml) tequila, the Triple Sec and lime juice. Mix well. Evenly pour over the poked cake, filling the holes as much as possible. Place the covered cake in the refrigerator for 2 to 4 hours or until the pudding is set.

COMBINE the whipped topping and the remaining 1 tablespoon (15 ml) of tequila in a large bowl until well combined. Evenly spread the whipped topping mixture over the cake. Garnish with the lime slices and zest. Refrigerate for at least 4 hours before serving.

STORE covered in the refrigerator.

bahama mama poke cake

This tropical cake is inspired by the adult drink of the same name. A pineapple-orange cake is soaked with rum and topped off with a cranberry-orange topping. Drink umbrellas optional.

PREP TIME: 10 MINUTES + CHILLING
COOK TIME: 35 MINUTES
YIELD: 18-24 SERVINGS

1 (15.25-oz [432-g]) box pineapple supreme cake mix

1 cup (240 ml) rum

1½ cups (480 g) orange marmalade

¾ cup (170 g) butter, softened

3 cups (375 g) powdered sugar

1 tbsp (6 g) orange zest

2–3 tbsp (30–45 ml) milk

¾ cup (83 g) fresh cranberries, finely chopped

PREPARE and bake the cake according to package directions, using a 13 x 9-inch (33 x 23-cm) cake pan. Let the cake cool for 15 to 20 minutes. Using the round end of a wooden spoon, poke holes in the cake every ½ inch (1.3 cm) to 1 inch (2.5 cm).

POUR the rum over the top of the cake. Evenly spread the marmalade over the cake. Use the back of a spoon to help push the marmalade into the poked holes. Refrigerate the cake for 8 hours or overnight.

BEAT the butter, powdered sugar, orange zest and milk in a large bowl until well combined and the frosting is light and fluffy. Add the cranberries and mix well. Spread the frosting over the cake. Refrigerate for at least 4 hours before serving.

STORE covered in the refrigerator.

bourbon sweet potato spice poke cake

Spice cake is infused with a hint of sweet potato and bourbon for the perfect grown-up poke cake.

PREP TIME: 10 MINUTES + CHILLING
COOK TIME: 35 MINUTES
YIELD: 18–24 SERVINGS

1 (15.25-oz [432-g]) box spice cake mix

2 (3.4-oz [96-g]) packages vanilla instant pudding mix

2 (4-oz [113-g]) containers sweet potato baby food

3 cups (700 ml) cold milk

½ cup (120 ml) bourbon

1 (8-oz [227-g]) tub frozen whipped topping, thawed

1 cup (110 g) toasted pecans, chopped

PREPARE and bake the cake according to package directions, using a 13 x 9-inch (33 x 23-cm) cake pan. Let the cake cool for 15 to 20 minutes. Using the round end of a wooden spoon, poke holes in the cake every ½ inch (1.3 cm) to 1 inch (2.5 cm).

EMPTY the pudding mix into a medium-sized bowl, add the baby food, milk and bourbon. Whisk briskly for 2 minutes or until the pudding is dissolved. Evenly pour over the poked cake, filling the holes as much as possible. Place the covered cake in the refrigerator for 2 to 4 hours or until the pudding is set.

SPREAD the whipped topping evenly over the cake. Use the back of a spoon or an offset spatula to spread it evenly. Sprinkle the pecans over the top. Refrigerate for at least 2 hours before serving.

STORE covered in the refrigerator.

sweet & salty pretzel poke cake

Whether you are craving something sweet—or something salty—this poke cake is sure to fit the bill. Chocolate cake marries with sweet caramel and plenty of pretzel pieces.

PREP TIME: 10 MINUTES + CHILLING
COOK TIME: 35 MINUTES
YIELD: 18–24 SERVINGS

1 (15.25-oz [432-g]) box chocolate cake mix

1 (14-oz [397-g]) can sweetened condensed milk

1 (11-oz [312-g]) jar caramel sauce

1 (8-oz [227-g]) tub frozen whipped topping, thawed

1 cup (160 g) chocolate-covered pretzels, roughly chopped

½ cup (56 g) pretzel sticks, roughly chopped

PREPARE and bake the cake according to package directions, using a 13 x 9-inch (33 x 23-cm) cake pan. Let the cake cool for 15 to 20 minutes. Using the round end of a wooden spoon, poke holes in the cake every ½ inch (1.3 cm) to 1 inch (2.5 cm).

MIX the sweetened condensed milk and caramel sauce in a large bowl until well combined. Evenly pour over the poked cake, filling the holes as much as possible. Place the covered cake in the refrigerator for 2 to 4 hours.

SPREAD the whipped topping over the top of the cake. Use the back of a spoon or an offset spatula to spread it evenly. Sprinkle the chocolate covered pretzels and pretzel sticks evenly over the top. Refrigerate for at least 2 hours before serving.

STORE covered in the refrigerator.

ACKNOWLEDGMENTS

To my husband, Brian—thank you for always being my biggest fan. You truly are my best friend and I know that none of this would be possible without your love and support. You encourage me to dream bigger than what I can dream on my own. You are the constant source of reason when I am discouraged. Your love and encouragement has helped me through so many days. I can't imagine my life without you and I am so thankful that we get to do this together. I love you!

To my kids, Elijah, Isaac, Thomas, Gabriel and Abby—you are the best things to ever happen to me. My heart bursts with love for you. Thank you for putting up with my numerous science experiments in the kitchen and for always being willing guinea pigs for my new recipes! I hope that I have shown you that you can do anything you want to do in life as long as you're willing to work hard.

To my parents—who would I be without you? You showed me through example that with hard work and determination, anything is possible. You taught me to be open-minded and encouraged me to be willing to try new things. You afforded me many opportunities that paved the way to any and all successes I've enjoyed in my life. Your sacrifices...I understand them all now that I have kids of my own, and I can never thank you enough. Thank you for your guidance. Thank you for letting me fail sometimes. Thank you for being there to pick me up and dust me off, and for helping get me back on track after those failures. Thank you for believing in me and giving me the foundation to succeed in life. Most of all, thank you for loving me. I also want to note that I've come a long way since those first "hockey puck" chocolate chip cookies!

To my grandma—I miss you every day. Thank you for letting a little girl with red hair watch you in the kitchen, and for letting her help. I have so many fond memories of family and food. Your kitchen is where I first had the desire to cook. If Heaven has a kitchen, I know you will be there with a big pot of your chili waiting for me. I love you!

To my blogger friends—thank you for being one of the most awesome communities ever. I had no idea what I was getting myself into when I started blogging and the bloggers I have met online or in real life have been outstanding and amazing people! You all have so much talent and I love that we are able to share with each other the things that we have learned along the way. Thank you for the opportunities to build each other up and to help each other out. I am humbled to be a part of such a wonderful group of people. I've met many of you in real life and I hope to meet so many more of you! Keep rockin' it!

To my blog readers and fans—where do I start? You are the reason I do what I do. I appreciate each and every person who has helped make Love Bakes Good Cakes what it is today—I couldn't have done it without you! From the bottom of my heart, thank you!

To Page Street Publishing—thank you for this amazing opportunity!

Last but not least, I thank God for giving me more blessings than I deserve.

ABOUT THE AUTHOR

Jamie Sherman is the jack-of-all-trades behind Love Bakes Good Cakes, a food blog that focuses on family-friendly recipes, including everything from healthier meal choices to over-the-top desserts! Since February 2012, Jamie has continued fine tuning her skills as a recipe developer, photographer and social media manager. Her work has been featured on numerous online sites including Foodgawker, All You, MSN, BuzzFeed, Huffington Post, Walmart, Country Living, Woman's Day, Delish, PopSugar, PEOPLE, Mr. Food, PARADE Community Table and many more.

Prior to being a food blogger, Jamie held jobs as a quality control lab technician for a large grain-processing company, an early learning educator and, for a period of time, as a school bus driver as well. In addition to food blogging, Jamie spends her days with her husband, Brian, and homeschooling 4 of their 5 children in the Phoenix area. She can also add grandma to her list, as she was blessed recently with her first grandbaby. When she has a minute of downtime, you can find her binge watching Netflix, reorganizing her kitchen and pantry for the umpteenth time, traveling or enjoying a fruity beverage by the pool.

INDEX